T0322045

EX LIBRIS

VINTAGE CLASSICS

LEN HOWARD

Len Howard (1894–1973) was a British naturalist and musician best known for her studies of birds, published as *Birds as Individuals* (1952) and *Living with Birds* (1956).

In her early life, Howard pursued a career in music in London, giving music lessons, organising concerts for the children of the poor and playing the viola professionally in an orchestra under Malcolm Sargent. In 1938, she purchased a plot of land outside the village of Ditchling, Sussex, and built the house she called Bird Cottage. There she developed an intimate and unusual relationship with the wild birds in the area, providing food (including her own war rations), chasing away predators, tending to damaged nests, and allowing the birds to fly and roost throughout her home. Her musical training gave her a unique insight into the diverse character of birdsong. Howard died at Bird Cottage in 1973.

LEN HOWARD

BIRDS AS INDIVIDUALS

WITH AN INTRODUCTION BY
Stephen Moss

VINTAGE CLASSICS

AUTHOR'S NOTE

Thanks are due to the editors of *Countrygoer* and *Out of Doors* for permission to reprint some sections of the Bird Biographies, etc. Also I wish to express my sincere thanks to Dr Julian Huxley for writing a foreword and for the interest he has shown. The majority of the photographs were especially taken for this book at Bird Cottage and I am much indebted to Eric Hosking for making two visits to my cottage to photograph the birds.

1 3 5 7 9 10 8 6 4 2

Vintage Classics is part of the Penguin Random House group of companies whose addresses can be found at global.penguinrandomhouse.com

Penguin
Random House
UK

This edition published in Vintage Classics in 2024
First published in Great Britain by Collins in 1952

Illustrated with photographs by Eric Hosking

penguin.co.uk/vintage-classics

Typeset in 10.5/12.5pt Bembo Book MT Pro by Jouve (UK), Milton Keynes
Printed and bound in Great Britain by Clays Ltd, Elcograf S.p.A.

The authorised representative in the EEA is Penguin Random House Ireland, Morrison Chambers, 32 Nassau Street, Dublin D02 YH68

A CIP catalogue record for this book is available from the British Library

ISBN 9781784879334

Penguin Random House is committed to a sustainable future for our business, our readers and our planet. This book is made from Forest Stewardship Council® certified paper.

Contents

Introduction

When I first heard about *Birds as Individuals*, written by Len Howard, I made the careless assumption that the author was a man. I later discovered that 'Len' was simply a shortened version of Gwendolen, her given name. But I do wonder if, like the nineteenth-century novelist George Eliot (born Mary Ann Evans), Howard deliberately chose a more masculine moniker. Perhaps it was her way of circumventing the ubiquitous climate of sexism towards women writers, which lasted throughout her lifetime and beyond.

Another contemporary naturalist and writer, S. Vere Benson, also never used her first name (Stephana), and likewise, was often assumed to be male. Vere Benson's best-known work, *The Observer's Book of Birds*, was first published in 1937, and became one of the bestselling bird books of the twentieth century – and for me, and many others of my generation, our first bird guide.

Yet Len Howard did not achieve such worldly success or fame. Her two published works (this 1952 book *Birds as Individuals* was followed, four years later, by *Living with Birds*), achieved modest sales, and received little notice in the press. One notable exception was from an anonymous reviewer in *Spectator* magazine, who wrote that 'Miss Howard's book of bird observation is the most remarkable I have ever read.'

Author Keggie Carew featured Howard's life and work in her 2023 book *Beastly: The Epic 40,000-Year Story of Animals and Us*. Carew believes that her intimate and detailed long-term studies were never really given the credit they deserve, despite their astonishing findings and the originality of her approach:

> One of her great tits lived for nine years, debunking the belief that they might have three years if they were lucky. Her musician's ear was the perfect tool for picking up their slightest inflections and she was so attentive to every nuanced behaviour.

Perhaps there is another reason why Howard's books did not become bestsellers. Unlike today, when bookshop tables are heaving with the latest crop of 'new nature-writing' volumes, the post-war period – and indeed most of the second half of the last century – was hardly a golden age for writing about the natural world.

There were plenty of scientific studies – including the celebrated New Naturalist series, also from Howard's publisher Collins, which was hugely popular amongst a post-war public eager to learn more about nature. This period also saw the first true 'field guides', including the 'birdwatcher's bible', *A Field Guide to the Birds of Britain and Europe* (also from Collins). But works of what we would now call 'creative non-fiction' – narratives with the author placed at the centre of the work – were few and far between.

For example, although written in the 1940s, *The Living Mountain*, by Howard's near-contemporary Nan Shepherd, was not published until 1977, shortly before the author's death. This demonstrates how Len Howard truly was ahead of her time.

Not until the early years of the current century did women nature-writers finally attain their long-deserved equal status with men. Having been excluded for so long, they soon began to dominate the genre: works such as *H is for Hawk* by Helen Macdonald, *The Outrun* by Amy Liptrot, and *Wilding* by Isabella Tree topping the bestseller lists as well as winning literary awards.

Birds as Individuals is certainly very different from today's nature writing. It reads like a cross between a diary and a textbook: the prose is unadorned, the tone brisk and the approach matter-of-fact. Indeed at times it feels as if the reader is being lectured by a rather strict (but deeply knowledgeable) schoolteacher.

And although Howard does give us an insight into her domestic life (notably the messy chaos resulting from allowing wild creatures inside her home), this is always subservient to the birds themselves, which are right at the heart of her writing. She clearly gained a great deal of pleasure from her relationship with them; yet her focus is never on her own innermost thoughts and feelings, but always on the life and behaviour of each individual bird.

This is just one of several aspects that make her work so interesting and valuable today, more than seventy years after it was first written and published.

★

Born in Wallington, Surrey in 1894, towards the end of Queen Victoria's long reign, Len Howard was raised in a family steeped in literature and culture: her father, (Henry) Newman Howard, was a published poet and dramatist. From an early age she showed a gift for music, and after leaving school she gave music lessons, played the viola in an orchestra and organised concerts for children from poor and deprived backgrounds.

In 1938, a year before the start of the Second World War, Howard purchased a plot of land just outside the Sussex village of Ditchling, on the South Downs north of Brighton. Here, she built a small house, which she named Bird Cottage, where she lived for the remaining three decades of her life.

Yet until she moved to Sussex – by then in her mid-forties – she had not shown much interest in the specific details of bird behaviour, as she herself confessed:

> When I first came to Bird Cottage I had not before been able to study bird behaviour for myself, although in London the libraries had supplied me with much bird literature. I was not expecting much intelligence to be shown . . .

But one spring morning, just three months after she had settled in, a single incident changed the course of Len Howard's life. As she was busily going about her household tasks, a blue tit entered through the open door:

> She hovered agitatedly close in front of me, her eyes fixed on mine, crying as I had never heard a Blue Tit cry before; it was at once obvious something was wrong and she was asking for my help.

Howard went outside to investigate and discovered that the birds' nest – complete with a dozen tiny eggs – had been pulled out of their nestbox, presumably by a local cat. With no time to waste, she gathered up the nesting material and eggs and carefully placed them back into the box. To her surprise, ten days later the whole clutch hatched, and the brood ultimately fledged successfully.

Her conclusion was that the distressed bird had quite deliberately sought her out for help – something she herself admitted was shamelessly anthropomorphic, in that she clearly attributed human emotions to its unusual behaviour. Going one step further, she also gave her birds names, enabling her to recall individuals. And she broke down the barriers between herself and the natural world by effectively creating an 'open house' for the birds, as Keggie Carew notes:

> When the great tits wanted to peck at her butter dish, normally forbidden, they looked at the butter, then up at her face, then at the butter. If she said 'Come on', coaxingly, they helped themselves, if she said 'No', firmly, they kept away. An angrier 'No!' could make them fly to the window.

Anyone who has ever owned a dog will be familiar with this kind of human–animal dynamic, yet like the Austrian zoologist Konrad Lorenz, Howard managed to achieve it with wild – or more accurately habituated – birds.

However, then, as they might still be now, scientists were highly suspicious of her informal and apparently haphazard approach. As Julian Huxley, at the time one of Britain's leading evolutionary biologists, noted in his conclusion to the book's foreword:

> Miss Howard will not expect professional biologists to accept all her conclusions. But they will be grateful for her facts; and I, personally, can testify to the enjoyment and interest her book has provided.

Despite this hint of scepticism, Huxley went on to praise Howard for her extraordinarily detailed observations. He also noted that by gaining the confidence of her garden birds, and losing their innate fear, she was able 'to be let into the secrets of their lives, and discover the degree of their intelligence'.

That she even gave up some of her meagre supplies of food – both during and after the war (food rationing continued until the early 1950s) – is a testimony to Howard's dedication to her feathered friends. And it worked: the birds soon lost their fear of humans – or more accurately they lost their fear of *her* – which allowed her to gain a deep insight into their lives, that few others have ever managed to achieve.

To maintain their trust, she became something of a recluse, rarely allowing visitors to enter her home. She even put up a typically blunt warning sign to deter any casual passers-by:

NO VISITORS
NESTING BIRDS
MUST KEEP COTTAGE QUIET
NO CALLERS

Yet when she reluctantly allowed someone to enter the hallowed portal, usually for purely practical reasons, she – and they – were richly rewarded, as she recounts in the opening chapter of her book:

> I always remember the words of an electrician who once called to attend to fittings in my Sussex cottage. He stopped in amazement before my doorway, watching countless birds flying down from the trees to perch on me . . . Then his whole countenance seemed to alter, his face glowed, his eyes shone and he kept murmuring: 'How wonderful!'

As her relationship with the birds deepened, Howard began to develop her theory that their behaviour was not governed solely by instinct, but was also shaped by their individual intelligence.

She was not alone in suggesting this: two very eminent ornithologists, Alexander Skutch and Bernd Heinrich, both concluded that birds are not mere automatons, and are far more intelligent than we usually give them credit for. Each of them published well-received books – Skutch's *The Minds of Birds* (1996) and Heinrich's *Mind of the Raven* (1999) – which contain many examples of complex behavioural traits that seem to go way beyond our usual perception of birds being, well, 'bird-brained'.

Yet for me, the fascinating questions about birds' intelligence raised by Len Howard's writing are trumped by something far simpler and yet more urgent: the population declines of so many once-common species since she first made her observations, back in the 1950s.

My own passion for birds began a decade or so later, as a young child. So I am fascinated by the changes in status of the bird visitors to her Sussex garden and its surroundings, which have happened in a mere two generations since she made her observations.

Several species that Howard considered commonplace are now either very scarce or have virtually disappeared from Sussex, and from much of the rest of southeast England. She writes of a pair of spotted flycatchers nesting just outside her window; of flocks of not just house sparrows but also tree sparrows; of corn buntings and house martins – all of whose numbers have fallen dramatically. And birds that were once so common that they are deeply ingrained in our nation's folklore, culture and literature – notably the cuckoo and the nightingale – have also vanished from much of our lowland countryside.

We don't need to be told the reasons for this. The dramatic declines in insects are primarily the result of modern industrial farming, as revealed in the work of Professor Dave Goulson, just down the road from Ditchling at the University of Sussex. These have combined with more unpredictable weather patterns as a result of the climate crisis, including a higher frequency of droughts, floods and other extreme weather events.

Together, these are reducing populations of birds we once took for granted to a mere remnant of what Len Howard would have known and enjoyed. The record she set down of the ordinary birds in a single garden in the middle of the twentieth century vividly highlights their decline. The stark comparison between then and now is perhaps the greatest legacy of her diaries and observations and one which, of course, she could never have imagined.

Gwendolen Howard died at Bird Cottage on 5 January 1973, in her eightieth year. For almost half a century afterwards she was more or less forgotten. But during the past decade or so her books and articles have been rediscovered and celebrated by a new generation of nature writers.

And now, thanks to this Vintage Classics edition, Len Howard's work can be read and enjoyed again by a new generation of naturalists and writers, who will surely enjoy reading her extraordinary accounts, observations and comments about our familiar – yet always fascinating – garden birds.

Stephen Moss, 2024

Foreword

Miss Howard has given us an unusual book. It is unusual because there are very few people in existence who love birds as much as she does, who have given so much time to watching them at such close quarters, and have taken the trouble to make notes of what they have seen and produce a book out of them.

Her title indicates one of the main points of interest that she brings out. When one watches birds day by day, year in and year out, one gets to know them individually, and finds that the behaviour of individuals differs much more than most people would suppose. I commend Miss Howard's observations on this point to my professional biological colleagues as well as to the general public.

A second point of interest is the way in which fear inhibits normality of behaviour. Only when birds have come to lose their fear, can a human observer really begin to be let into the secrets of their lives, and discover the degree of their intelligence. This point too is one to be taken to heart by professional biologists.

Finally, Miss Howard has paid a great deal of attention to the songs of her birds, and since she is a professional musician, her observations and conclusions are of more than ordinary interest and value. I was particularly struck by her account of the cock Blackbird who composed (the word is Miss Howard's, and seems appropriate) a phrase almost identical with the opening phrase of the Rondo in Beethoven's Violin Concerto. At any rate, he gradually worked it up from a simple beginning.

Miss Howard has a stimulating and entertaining chapter on play in birds, and gives us a number of incidental observations of considerable interest, such as the relaxation of territorial rivalry and aggressiveness during a period of drought.

Miss Howard will not expect professional biologists to accept all her conclusions. But they will be grateful for her facts; and I, personally, can testify to the enjoyment and interest her book has provided.

Julian Huxley

Part One

BIRD BEHAVIOUR

CHAPTER I

Preliminary: Confidence,
Sense and Intelligent Behaviour

A great many people have shown interest in my tame-wild birds. Often strangers see me with them perched on my hand down the road and stop to ask how it is these birds have got so tame. In this 'better world' now being planned for future generations will it still be so rare to see the beautiful wild birds perching fearlessly on human hands? I always remember the words of an electrician who once called to attend to fittings in my Sussex cottage. He stopped in amazement before my doorway, watching countless birds flying down from the trees to perch on me. He had looked an ordinary man with a work-a-day expression until he saw these birds, then his whole countenance seemed to alter, his face glowed, his eyes shone and he kept murmuring: 'How wonderful!' Then he said: 'But why shouldn't it be like that? It ought to be like that.'

There are, of course, great difficulties in living as I do, in continual company of numbers of birds. The practical ones are many, such as cleaning up, having things spoilt, the rooms always looking as if prepared for the sweep with newspapers spread over furniture and books covered with cloths: then the disturbance of sleep, for they hammer furiously on the panes if I shut the windows at dawn to keep them outside when the nights are short, and they do all they can to prevent my concentrating upon anything except themselves. But there are even worse problems. Living with birds, it is impossible not to get fond of each individual. But their lives are short and there are many tragedies. There is the havoc wrought by cats unless I am continually on the watch. Bird Cottage is not in an isolated position; it is built in a strip of old farm orchard at one end of a fairly large village in Sussex. This farm was converted into several private properties so these houses are around mine, besides others that have sprung up over the way. But the garden is well secluded by trees and tall hedges, and I leave much of it to grow half-wild in its own graceful way, with briars, may-trees, wild plum and elder seeding themselves, and thick ivy clambering up the tall stumps of old apple and pear trees. These provide food and cover for the birds, the ivy berries especially useful as they ripen at a time when other food is often scarce through frost. Around my boundaries I let the grass grow high during the nesting season. This gives cats more trouble to find entrance when it is wet with dew or rain; but nothing that I do will keep them away.

Then there are the Jackdaws and Magpies that steal young birds. Magpies have become far too plentiful and have practically wiped out the Marsh- and Coal-Tits in this neighbourhood. My birds rely upon me to keep away all these plunderers. Most mornings recently I have been awakened at five o'clock by a Great Tit making agitated flights to and fro from my bed to the window while uttering loud alarm cries. He is telling me to come out quickly, the Magpie is endangering his young, so I leap from bed and chase off this enemy with a stick. I return to bed, but soon there is more trouble, the Blackbird calls me up by agitated 'tchinks' close to my window, and again I go out to frighten away the cat by flinging a jug of water at it with a big splash. It slinks off through the bushes, of course avoiding getting wet. In spite of all my efforts some birds fall victims to the cats and Magpies. If I go on a holiday so many disasters occur that I very rarely go away, although wanting to watch other kinds of birds farther afield.

There are often injured ones among my many birds, dependent upon me for their recovery. In one way and another my birds demand attention from dawn until dusk. They do all they can to hinder any concentrated work, – while I am trying to write this page some are perching on the typewriter, some pulling at my hair, others flying to my hands and falling off as I start to tap the keys. There is one other person who knows from experience how demanding my Great Tits can be. This is a man named 'Old Harry,' who, like me, loves all the wild creatures. He lives in his own little hut in a spinney about ten minutes walk from my cottage. One of my Great Tits this year was crowded out of my garden and she nested in his spinney. Until her young were hatched she used to fly back to me every morning and evening, urgently demanding a good feed. Then this kind old man, who feeds the birds, became the victim of her imperious ways. 'Proper tart, she is,' said Old Harry; 'she calls me up at dawn by tugging at the blankets and pecking at my face. You can't stop her and you've got to give her all she wants, and quickly too.' I knew at once from his description which bird it was, for this was exactly how the little tart had always treated me.

Perhaps it is because of my intense love for birds that they come to me quickly and I have not found any difficulty in gaining their confidence. Directly I moved into Bird Cottage I put up a bird-table and bath close to the french window, and a Robin, Blue Tit and Blackbird came at once, many more species, including the Great Tit, soon following. I have always talked to my birds in a normal speaking voice, for they soon learn to understand something of speech by its tone. Very quickly this great intimacy developed and the numbers rapidly increased. Besides loving their company, I find immense interest in studying their individual characters and through this close intercourse I can reach a better understanding of their minds.

When I first came to Bird Cottage I had not before been able to study bird behaviour for myself, although in London the libraries had supplied me with much bird literature. I was not expecting much intelligence to be shown in their behaviour and was very surprised when the following incident occurred. It was a spring morning, three months after my little cottage had been built, and I was busy within, near an open door, when a Blue Tit came fluttering up with cries of distress. She hovered agitatedly close in front of me, her eyes fixed on mine, crying as I had never heard a Blue Tit cry before; it was at once obvious something was wrong and she was asking for my help. Her mate was with her but perched just outside, watching me intently. Directly I went out she stopped crying and they led me to her nesting-box, flying on in front and at suitable perches on the way, turning round to see that I followed. The whole of her nest had been pulled in fragments from the nesting-box and her twelve eggs lay scattered over the hard wooden floor of the box. The lid was shut, so it appeared a cat had clawed out the nest in pieces through the entrance hole. (From this experience I learnt that nest-boxes should be deeper than five inches.)

Both Tits waited close by, silently watching while I quickly gathered the fragments of nest from the ground, removed the eggs and re-formed the nest in the box as well as I could, then replaced the eggs on the right side of the box, thinking she would like it as near as possible the same as before. Directly I had finished the mother bird flew in, and after removing her eggs to the other side of the rather large box, brooded her clutch again. Ten days later the eggs hatched, and she brought off her brood in spite of the calamity because she had sensibly thought of appealing to me for help. What else except thought could have made her act thus? It is not a bird's instinct to seek man but avoid him over anything in connection with nesting affairs. I had not then been long in my cottage and no other bird had been helped over nesting difficulties or anything else. I had merely fed the birds and watched unseen while they built their nests. But many birds had grown very tame and they trusted me.

It had been interesting to watch this Blue Tit and her mate during nest-building. He had at first tried to interest her in a tree-stump hole, but she refused to pay much attention to this, the large nesting-box attached to another tree having taken her fancy. She spent much time popping in and out of this while he stood on the ledge outside, peering cautiously through the entrance hole or examining the lid and sides of the box. Then he started going inside with her and much eager-sounding twittering went on between them, with playfulness in their manner when he chased her out and around the trees, she again flying back to her chosen nesting-box. This went on for over a month before the first material was brought to the nest, not the usual moss or wool but packing-case shavings for foundation. She flew with the shavings into the nesting-box, he flying after her and watching through the entrance hole until she flew for more. Afterwards came moss and, finally, white horses' hair and feathers, the latter continuing to be added occasionally after the twelve eggs were laid. Her mate gave no practical help over the building, which took a month, but his enthusiasm for accompanying and watching her was equal to her evident pleasure in this work and his presence.

All Blue Tits do not show the same attachment for each other. It varies in degree and more often their behaviour, once nesting has started, is extremely quiet and secretive. I think this applies to the older, experienced birds, who have found it wiser, for this ecstatic couple afterwards adopted a comparatively quiet and sober caution directly nesting began.

Later that year two nestling Robins, before they were fledged, fell from their insecure nest in a shallow tree-hole. The remaining two were in danger of falling and the parents showed much concern. I put the four babies into a coconut shell, where they snuggled down contentedly, then I tied this improvised nest to the seat of a chair placed underneath the tree, surrounding the chair-seat with leafy twigs and covering it with sacking, only leaving a small hole for the parent Robins' entrance. They were meanwhile occupied on the nearby hedge, flitting about and 'tic-ticing' at my neighbour's cat. They appeared not to notice my interference, but Robins often turn their backs and look unconcerned when really interested. I retired, wondering if they would find their nestlings, especially through so small an opening, but they soon left the hedge and flew straight to the coconut nest although the babies were silent. The parents did not once return to their old nest, yet I had taken two babies from it. The young never attempted to leave their coconut nest until a week later when they were ready to fly.

I have no doubt the Blue Tits and Robins would not have behaved intelligently if they had feared my presence. Often bird behaviour is judged when the bird is panicked with fear of the watcher. But many humans would prefer not to have an intelligence test when they or their young are in probable danger of immediate death. I find the normal thing is for birds, especially Tits, to act intelligently in unusual circumstances unless they get flustered through fear.

I once half-raised the lid of a Blue Tit's nesting-box but, finding she was sitting, very quickly closed it again. She was alarmed, not having seen the lid opened before, and flew from the entrance hole straight to her mate who was at the other side of my cottage, and could not possibly have seen what had happened. They returned quickly together to the nest, she to continue brooding her eggs and he to behave exactly as if he knew the cause of her fright. First he examined the lid carefully, then looked at her through the entrance hole and after another inspection of the box, settled down on a narrow ledge outside the entrance hole, apparently to keep guard or give her confidence. Occasionally he put his head inside the nesting-box to look at her. He had never before behaved like this while she brooded. After about half an hour she came off to feed; he never again stayed outside while she was sitting – this would be against their natural behaviour for it would attract notice to the nest.

It seems evident that birds can communicate with each other by

slight inflections of voice and of movement, because I find those that
know me well understand much by their sensitive interpretation of
my voice or least movement. For example, when Great Tits want to
peck at my butter dish, which they know is usually forbidden, they
perch a little way off and look first at the butter, then at my face, hesitating although longing to help themselves, for they have a passion for
butter. If I say 'come on' coaxingly, they confidently step up and eat
it. If I say 'no' just a little sternly they remain where they are, but continue to look pleadingly at me and then at the butter. A shade crosser
'no' sends them hopping farther off; an angry 'no' makes them fly to
the open window, but if I quickly call out, 'Here, come on,' in a very
coaxing tone, they at once return and if I keep quiet, inch by inch they
hop along the table towards the butter, still eyeing me for further signs
of objection. Once on their guard by 'no' in the first place, they will
not step up with the airy confidence shown when I encourage them by
saying 'come on' at first. They interpret correctly any sign of objection in voice or movement, but without the encouraging tone of voice
they will not touch butter while I am looking because I have once or
twice forbidden them by an angry 'no.' Their extreme sensitiveness
makes them learn extraordinarily quickly. I have to know the bird
before communicating satisfactorily by voice inflection; strangers are
naturally uncertain through nervousness, but Great Tits generally
learn my meaning very soon.

Some Blackbirds, and a few other individuals to a lesser degree, I
have found sensitive in the same way. A Blackbird from next door
(called Thief and referred to in Chapter 3) once got the better of me in
his characteristic manner after he had been obeying nicely like the Tits
in the above butter dish example. Bread and potatoes had been the
only food allowed him for all the obedience and intelligence he had
shown, while on my knee was a plate containing meat – my lunch and
about half the week's ration! Suddenly Thief threw all discretion to
the winds and flew up under my very nose, snatched the whole slice of
meat from the plate in my lap and was over the hedge with a chuckle-
note before I had time to object or realise what had happened. Among
Blackbirds, only Thief with his pick-pocket action would dare, and
accomplish successfully, such theft from under my nose.

Great Tits sometimes commit similar thefts when they see I am
thinking of something else. As well as interpreting voice inflections

and movements, they appear to know a great deal by watching eyes and facial expressions, for I notice when looking at them with thoughts absorbed elsewhere they act as if my back is turned and then commit sins they never dare when I am looking consciously at them, watching and thinking of them.

Watching birds closely and intimately, there are continual actions that cannot be accounted for by instinct and automatic reaction, but intelligence varies much with the individual as well as the species, and of the birds with which I am intimately acquainted, Great Tits reach the highest level of intelligence, consequently also of individuality within the species.

Some people are under the delusion that Great Tits are cruel to other birds because of the late Viscount Grey of Fallodon's story of the Great Tit who ate the Sparrow's brains when both were trapped in a cage. During ten years of constant observation of the Great Tit I have not seen one act of cruelty committed by this species. Sparrows frequently bully other birds, Great Tits included, and the Great Tit does not even hit back. He merely spreads his wings in a display of protest and then flies off, for he is a good-tempered bird and normally does not fight other species. It is unfair to judge a bird when frenzied by captivity and starvation. Great Tits have tremendous vitality and the Tit may have outlived the Sparrow in the cage and had the sense to save himself from starvation by a meal off the dead bird's brain. If he did kill the Sparrow probably the latter, as is his custom, began the fight and the Great Tit, being in captivity, could not retreat as he does when free. Blue Tits are more pugnacious with other species than Great Tits. It is amusing to watch a Blue Tit attacking a Great Tit, who usually only displays in return, showing remarkable tolerance for his small relation. I have seen a Blue Tit attack a Blackbird who pecked at the Tit's suet which had fallen from its usual suspended position. The Blackbird retorted by lifting the Blue Tit on his beak and tossing him a couple of feet away, as if the Tit was no more than a leaf. The Blackbird then continued to eat the suet with his back turned to the sprawling Blue Tit who soon picked himself up and flew away.

During autumn and winter for the last three years there has been a daily episode at dusk in my cottage. A Blue Tit flutters through the sitting-room, hesitatingly because of the dim light, and flies to the sliding doors that separate my two rooms. They have been left open for her, and she wants to slip through a very narrow crevice between the runner of the doors and the beam. She flutters her wings while trying to gain a foothold, but often fails on her first attempt. She retires to a chair-back for a moment, then tries again, her wings beat vigorously as she steadies herself and slowly squeezes her small body through the slit into a recess above the beam – a spacious bedroom for a Blue Tit. If the doors are closed at her bedtime she flies up to me with a whimpering cry, and I open them for her; when she is inside the recess they can be pulled across; she taps on the beam to be let out if they are shut when she awakens at dawn. Sometimes she oversleeps, the doors are open and I am drawing back the window curtains before she is up, then she quickly slips from her roost – getting out being easy – and flies to the window, still sleepy-looking and flying as if half-awake. Once out in the open, she is all life and energy in her movements and starts her day by a vigorous preen on the trees near my window. She has taken such a fancy to this roost that she was not put off even when last year she took a wrong turning from bed one morning and fell over the back end of the door, getting trapped in unknown dark regions, this necessitating my fetching a builder to release her. She was unperturbed and returned the next night as usual. This autumn her mate flutters behind her to the sliding doors at dusk; he is at present a beginner at manœuvring the crevice, and has many failures before he gains a roost near her on the inside beam.

CHAPTER 2

Bird Biography: Great Tits

I

Watching the nesting affairs of birds in my garden has shown much variety of behaviour within the species, especially among Great Tits. It is consistent with their greater intelligence that their behaviour should differ more. Although I have found that they mate for life, some seem indifferent to each other's company except during the nesting season, other couples keep together always, and if they lose sight of their mate for a few minutes an alert expression and fixed posture is maintained until the mate reappears. If one mate of these devoted couples dies the successor is regarded comparatively with indifference, sometimes even during nesting season. In these cases I have seen of special devotion, they have been young birds, not previously mated. The same applies to other species.

There are various ways by which I recognise my Great Tits individually. They are easier to distinguish than most species. Having such close contact with them, I get to know their different facial expressions and characteristic mannerisms and poses. Also, there are considerable variations in their frontal attire and sometimes in the shape of their white facial markings, or there may be slight differences in the tone-colourings of their plumage. But the birds that figure prominently in the following biographies I was able to recognise even if their plumage was darkened and disordered by being wet after their bath, and therefore bereft of any distinguishing marks. Their whole bearing and personality was too individual for confusion to arise when I had them at close quarters. Generally, the same markings of plumage are kept after the moult, except, of course, the fledgling moult and change to adult plumage. But when the young are in moult I am able to follow day by day the changes that occur, for those with whom I am intimate are so frequently on my hand or lap, as also are their parents.

One female Great Tit was under my close observation for six years.

She was reared in my neighbour's orchard and mated a bird of the same age from my garden. They reared two broods each year for three years and were a devoted pair, always together, even in winter. If one appeared at my window without the other, the bird would stay motionless and seem oblivious of tempting food offered it until the mate was in sight. Usually they entered and left my room together.

This female, called Jane, had the originality to sing a charming song during nesting season. Her gift was unique. Other female Great Tits do not sing although they have a variety of call-notes, a scold-note, etc.; but Jane's song was much superior to the male's. It varied a little from year to year and in these first years of her life it slightly resembled the male's 'tee-chū' song, but was much more musical. Instead of repetition of the same notes, she dropped down the scale in overlapping approximate thirds. The song was begun in gay, ringing tones and gradually grew softer and sweeter as it lowered in pitch. A chime of bells dying away on the wind was suggested.

The fourth year Jane's mate died of an injured leg. She mated another first-year bird, in appearance resembling her other mate, who was of exceptionally large build, with broader frontal markings than usual. She nested that spring in a tree trunk down the road, having been driven from her usual site in my garden by a pugnacious couple of Great Tits who greedily wanted the whole garden to themselves. When Jane's first brood by mate II was fledged, she tried to bring them to my garden, but the pugnacious pair chased them away. Even if I tried to give her food by the stream across the road, the pugnacious male would flash over my hedge with angry demonstrations to prevent Jane and mate II from taking food from my hand for their young. But while her second brood were nestlings, mate II was killed by a cat. She carried on feeding her young with increased effort and I often saw her pause on the threshold of her nest after leaving it, a worried expression on her face;[*] then she would fly to the tree-top and glance in all directions as if looking for her mate. As soon as her brood flew she again brought them to my garden. This time neither of the pugnacious Tits showed objection, although

_____

[*] This may appear anthropomorphic, but her whole manner as well as her look showed she was worried. In my dose observations of the tits I have learnt to tell by their looks and manner if they are troubled about something, and I am satisfied that in this instance it was the case.

they still would not tolerate other Great Tits entering the garden, for they also had a second brood. Sometimes the pugnacious male, with food in his beak intended for his own nestlings, would stop and appear to listen to the noise Jane's eight hungry fledglings were making, and instead of taking the food to his nestlings he flew to one of the widow's young and popped the caterpillar down its throat.

The following year Jane mated another first-year bird, offspring of the pugnacious couple. Again she had chosen a mate of big build and dark frontal attire. He was a very interesting character and unique nesting affairs followed. For some time Jane had been vying with another female Great Tit, called Grey, for a large nesting-box hung to a tree in my orchard. In early April both began bringing moss to the box, each working when the other was absent, but I think Jane removed Grey's contribution, as when she entered the nest with her own material she often threw moss out of the nesting-hole. Grey never did this.

I was at that time puzzled because Grey appeared to have no mate and lived either alone or with Jane and her mate III. A few days later I saw Jane enter the nest with Grey following. They remained together in the nest for several minutes, both making the continuous high-pitched noise, resembling nestling-cries, that is used by Great Tits in certain phases of nesting. Then they flew out together amicably. This happened many times while Jane completed her nest. Grey had now stopped bringing material.

Mate III was occupied meanwhile in strenuous song and defending the tree from intruders, which cost him his crown feathers. Henceforth he was called Baldhead. He occasionally went inside the nesting-box, as if to see how things were progressing. I have never seen any male Great Tit or Blue Tit help with nest-building, although many attentive males escort their mates backwards and forwards to the nest while material is being collected by the female. This attention of the male occurs in many species and gives a false impression that the male is also building.

Jane's delightful little song, now more original than ever, frequently rang through the orchard. She would fly from her nest to fetch more material, singing while she flew, as if with an overflow of happiness. Grey, like a silent shadow, would often fly after her.

When Jane laid her first egg, Grey was no longer allowed entrance to the nesting-box. With great rapidity she then built a nest for herself in another box in the orchard, a beautiful one woven in many colours, for she had tugged away at my rugs, coats and coloured blankets and flown out of the window with beakfuls of bright, fluffed-up wool. But I had not the heart to stop this destruction, for I knew she was in a desperate hurry. I had then found out that Jane's mate was also hers. With equal devotion, Baldhead guarded both of their nesting sites, followed them about, and inspected their nests. The females were still friendly and the three went about together. In three days Grey's nest was completed and her first egg laid. Baldhead attentively fed both his mates, on their nests when they were sitting and when they were off – which was often at the same time. Both fluttered their wings before him while uttering baby-cries, and in turn he fed them, always in a gallant manner and showing no favouritism. Sometimes he fed Grey in the trees near Jane's nest when she was sitting. There must have been a spy-hole in her nesting-box, for she always appeared to see this and, apparently to attract attention, she would sing her little song several times from her nest, afterwards popping her head out of the nesting-hole a few times, as if impatient. Grey waited her turn patiently when conditions were reversed.

On May 8th Jane's young started hatching, and from the day that Baldhead began feeding her nestlings, Grey was completely deserted. She fluttered her wings before him and made baby-cries as before, but he ignored her. On May 11th Grey's young also began to hatch. When off her nest she followed Baldhead to Jane's nesting-box with excited cries and wing quiverings. (This appeared to be giving information that nestlings were hatching.) Her mate still took no notice and Jane chased her away. She seemed greatly distressed, making queer cries and scolding-notes as she returned to her nest. For the next day or two, whenever she saw Baldhead the same pathetic appeals were made with no success, and on May 14th she flew into my room just as he was taking cheese from me for Jane's nestlings. At once she stood still, quivering her wings and wailing more than ever. Baldhead suddenly eyed her curiously, and with the cheese still in his beak, mounted her, but she angrily spread her tail and shook him off. He flew away and never again took notice of her. I enticed him to Grey's nest and made him look at the nestlings. He gazed at them a moment but flew off to Jane's nest, never returning to Grey's. Whenever the deserted mate saw Jane or Baldhead, she placed herself before them with distressed wailing and quiverings that grew more and more exaggerated and sometimes, when they had flown from sight, she would fly to my shoulder with wings still violently quivering and look up into my face with a pathetic, appealing expression. She had always fed from my hand and I was helping her with food for her nestlings but she would not eat anything for herself now. Her trouble was not to feed her young, for the female will carry on when her mate dies, as Jane had done when her second mate was killed, without expending energy on distressful display. Grey was apparently fretting at desertion.

On the morning of May 19th Grey did not come to me as usual to fetch food for her nestlings, but spent nearly all the time hovering near Jane's nest, with incessant exaggerated emotional display. It became very distressing to watch her, so agonised was her wailing cry and so pathetic her appearance as she kept quivering her wings with this unnatural effort. Even her nestlings were deserted while she made her last appeal. That afternoon she died, apparently of her grief. The nestlings survived only a few hours.

Jane and Baldhead brought off their brood and also reared a second one successfully, but Jane seemed very tired afterwards and never regained strength after her moult. She and Baldhead did not show special interest in each other during the winter, although they were often together. The sound of her wings in flight had altered and was heavier. She survived the hard winter, but died in early April, 1947, aged six.

2

Baldhead, even in his fledgling days, was an interesting bird of very definite character. His parents, the Pugnacious Tits, started preparations for a second brood two weeks after he was fledged, and Baldhead developed an unusual obsession for watching all the nesting affairs. Normally first brood Great Tits take no notice of the second brood (only some Great Tits are double-brooded). The rest of the fledglings never went near the nest, but Baldhead spent much time leaning over the nesting-hole, as if trying to solve the mystery of it all and why his father had suddenly taken to feeding his mother instead of him. When she came off her nest this inquisitive offspring would crane his head down the nesting-hole and stare at the eggs until she returned, often pushing him away and spreading her wings over the entrance in protest. Every day, as if magnetised by it, he returned again and again to the nesting-hole. It was funny to watch his start of surprise when gaping beaks first shot up at him from the nest. He drew back then ventured another look with head held first one side then the other, as if to make sure he was seeing correctly. It seemed the naked nestlings fascinated him; he continually stared at them, always starting back at first sight, when I presume their beaks shot up at him in expectation of food. He hindered the parents' work of feeding the babies, for when they took food to the nest he stuck his head down the entrance hole to watch, and the parents would come out with scolding notes to push him away. If they chased him he assumed baby ways, shivering his wings and making baby-cries. He rarely got caterpillars given him now, but he fed often from my hand and sometimes, while taking a favourite bit of cheese, he would look towards the nest then, dropping the cheese, hurriedly fly to it as if afraid of missing something that was going on down entertainment hole.

When the second brood flew and one fledgling was balancing uncertainly on a twig with the tendency to fall forward habitual to Great Tit babies on first perching, Baldhead flew up and went through an astonishing performance of Tit-antics in front of the baby, who stared at him with an expression of great interest. Having turned a somersault round a twig and hung on to it upside down with one foot, swinging the other in the air, also vigorously pulled off leaves and chucked them down, he finally hammered the bark with a loud tattoo then flew off, never again taking the slightest interest in the fledglings or the nesting-hole.

After Jane died in early April, Baldhead soon found another mate. She chose a new nesting-box on a tree in the orchard, but he showed no interest in this mate or her nest, and he rarely accompanied or fed her. He had now developed another obsession, this time for Grey's old nesting-box. With much display he had kept this from other Tits although he took no notice of Jane's old nests – for her second brood she had built in another nesting-box. Often when his new mate came off her eggs and called to him, expecting attention, he was absorbed in an excited performance with Grey's old nesting-box and ignored her. She waited nearby a moment, then her gentle call-note changed to a subdued scold-note as she flew away to fend for herself. Baldhead continued his frenzied behaviour over the empty nesting-box apparently without noticing his mate. She was called Monocle, one of her eyes having a rim, looking like an eyeglass. It is difficult to describe this queer behaviour because so much depended upon the excited manner and his absorption. He first peered through the entrance hole eagerly, as if expecting to see something, then with high-pitched nestling-cry sounds he entered the nest and worked up a great crescendo of urgent-sounding cries until he suddenly began hopping hurriedly in and out of the box, his movements getting quicker and quicker, as if his life depended upon the speed of this action. Occasionally he hopped on to the lid of the box with an odd little call, then back inside again, repeating the whole performance, although never in a set pattern. His frantic haste and urgent-sounding cries were abnormal behaviour. To a bird-watcher's eye his present mate, Monocle, had much less charm or individuality than Jane or Grey. Did Baldhead feel this and want Grey back in her old nest, or was he perhaps unsatisfied because this year he had only one mate? It is extremely unusual for Great Tits to be bigamists, but they have so much individuality that their nesting affairs have no set pattern, although it is more usual for them to have one brood and for the male to be attentive to his mate during egg-brooding, also to show enthusiasm over feeding the young, even two or three weeks after they have flown. But even these normal nesting affairs that are often termed 'instinctive' show great variation in detail and no two couples are quite alike in behaviour to each other while nest-building and rearing young.

Baldhead's frenzied performance over Grey's nest would cease suddenly, then he would fly off in a calm, leisurely manner in the opposite direction to his mate's nest. All this was very unlike his behaviour to the two mates the previous year. When they were both sitting, he fed them constantly, always accompanied them when off their nests and guarded their nesting sites with continual vigilance.

The obsession for Grey's nest lasted until his mate's eggs hatched, when he devoted himself to feeding his eight young. Also, he and his mate adopted eight young fledglings belonging to one of his and Jane's offspring.

It came about this way. One of Jane's second brood, called Fatty, was big and bold like his father and an interesting bird to watch. Like Baldhead, he remained in my garden all the year round and their nests were on adjoining territory. Baldhead possessed the orchard, Fatty and another couple shared the front garden. Baldhead and Fatty had many disputes over their boundary, with much display and odd language.

Their mates also had lively quarrels between themselves, sometimes rolling together on the ground with feet interlocked. The females' disputes were hot and sharp but quickly over, while the males appeared to enjoy making a prolonged game or fantastic art of their varied ways of displaying, sometimes for three hours at a stretch.

Fatty was a devoted mate, as so often with first-year birds. He accompanied his wife while she collected nesting material, watching all her movements though not helping practically. She pushed him out if he tried to follow her into the nest, so he waited outside patiently, with occasional glances through the nesting-hole, until she flew for more material. Perhaps the reason males of many species do not help with nest-building is that the females will not allow it.

One afternoon, while his mate rested on a branch above her nesting-box, Fatty ventured inside and made gentle nestling-cry sounds from the nest. She immediately flew to another tree and called to him. He joined her, and having got him off her nest she returned to the same branch above it, and perched on one foot, continued her rest. He flew to the nesting-box again, but this time stayed quietly on the ledge outside the entrance hole, often looking up at her.

On June 2nd poor Fatty lost his mate. There had been an intense heat-wave and she had seemed much exhausted while feeding her young through the heat. They were now within five or six days of flying, had things been normal. All that day and the next, Fatty carried on feeding the young, but seemed restless and unhappy. When he came as usual to my hand for food, each piece picked up was thrown down and, without eating anything, he flew away.

On June 4th he fed his young until 11 a.m., but his manner was strange and he looked absent-minded. He never came to my hand that morning – for the first time in his life he had taken no notice when I called him. Nor did he appear to see favourite tit-bits I held before his eyes – nuts and cheese that he had always before been eager to eat or take to his young. His eyes seemed not focusing upon anything close in front of him, and they had a strange expression. At eleven o'clock I went out and on returning at two-thirty I found Fatty had disappeared. The young cried ceaselessly until 5 p.m. Then Baldhead, no doubt attracted by their cries, looked at them through the entrance hole with an interested expression on his face, but he flew off again to feed his own young, who were fledged on May 31st and were still in the orchard.

Would Baldhead adopt Fatty's eight young if I gave them to him? The chances seemed small, for he had eight of his own, but I took two from the nest and placed them in his nesting-box. At once the bigger one scrambled out through the entrance hole, fortunately just as Monocle appeared. It fluttered to a nearby branch. Monocle looked puzzled, gave first a little scold-note then the gentle call-note used when young ones first fly. The hungry fledgling cried loudly and shivered its wings on seeing her. She glanced at the trees, apparently making sure no parents were coming, then she quickly fetched caterpillars several times, as if realising the fledgling's extreme hunger. She next went to her nesting-box and peered through the entrance hole. The other baby crouched silently in the nest but she did not enter. I placed it beside the first one on the branch. Being smaller and unable to fly properly it overbalanced and fell into the grass. Monocle showed much concern and hovered over it, calling in gentle tones, trying to coax it upwards to a safer perch. But it only cried, so she fed it in the grass.

I fetched two more of Fatty's babies. Baldhead arrived while I was placing them on the branch, beside the first fledgling. Like his mate, he looked bewildered at the sight of them near his nest. He first scanned the trees for parents, a scold-note, feebly begun, died away into silence and he looked at his mate, who exchanged his glance. She then turned to the fledglings and called gently. In a flash Baldhead disappeared and returned with a large caterpillar dangling from his beak, and although the young were not now crying he enthusiastically stuffed them with food, fetched at record speed. They both appeared to realise these young were starving although there were not now any outward signs that they were hungry.

All was going so well that I fetched the remaining four, two at a time. Baldhead and Monocle became more and more excited, calling and feeding them in a flustered manner and often exchanging glances. Then Baldhead flew to his nesting-box, his mate following, and with much subdued chattering, they examined the box behind, below and on top as well as inside, seemingly trying to account for these fledglings. As Baldhead had not seen them come from his nest it seemed his mate had communicated this to him.

By degrees they coaxed the bigger fledglings to join their own young on the trees across the orchard, but four were too small to fly properly and needed my assistance. So successful was this adoption that even more care was bestowed on them than their own fledglings. Baldhead seemed in his element with this excitement of adoption and even his behaviour to his mate altered. He now sought her company when she flew near their nest and they both displayed with vibrating wings, making nestling-cry imitations by the nest, which they had not done after their own young flew. This recapitulation of pre-nesting display, often with more emotion shown than before nesting, is usual with Great and Blue Tits whose nesting affairs have been carried on with enthusiasm. Although Baldhead had not displayed with Monocle after their own young flew, the previous year he and Jane had many wing-quivering displays after each of their broods had flown.

On June 29th, three weeks after Fatty's disappearance, he returned with three full-grown young, about five days younger than his own. He flew straight to his usual perch on my shoulder, then to my hand for food which he took to these adopted young. Some widow must have enticed him to help rear his family, but she did not appear with him in my garden.

Fatty's own young were by this time much reduced in number and being taught independence by their foster-parents. Because now seldom fed, they chased after Fatty instead, and tried to snatch caterpillars from his beak that were being taken to the adopted trio. Although he did not let them seize the food he was surprisingly good-tempered with these pestering youngsters, and never pushed them away with scold-notes as is usual when the full-grown young of one brood pester the parents taking food to another; but these clamouring young were Fatty's offspring and had more right to the caterpillars than the adopted trio. Whether Fatty realised this or not cannot be proved but, watching his tolerance when they persistently chased after him, it appeared that he did recognise his lawful young. They caused him so much trouble that he invented a clever dodge of taking the food a roundabout route through my cottage, these youngsters being less familiar with the bathroom and kitchen windows than he was. When one of his offspring was clever enough to follow this dodge he outwitted it by amazingly fast flight round trees, so the youngster only caught him up in time to see the coveted caterpillar being swallowed by one of the adopted trio.

Fatty had much to contend with on his return. Baldhead now seemed to bear him a grudge and fiercely chased him from the front garden whenever he saw him. As Baldhead's territory was the orchard at the back, this malice had nothing to do with territorial defence. The other Great Tits with young, whose nesting tree was in the front garden, never molested him, nor did Baldhead show anger to any other Great Tit except Fatty. By deserting his young, Baldhead seemed to consider he had forfeited the right to return to his nesting site and Fatty did not resist his angry demonstrations.

In the autumn a female — possibly the mother of the trio — often accompanied Fatty to the cottage and gradually Baldhead ceased to molest him, except that on very mild October and November days Fatty was attacked if he looked inside any of the nesting-boxes in the garden. He never nested here again, but is often with me out of nesting season.

Baldhead and his mate kept together during autumn and winter, although not showing much interest in each other. They had some disputes over new roosting-boxes put up for them. Baldhead expected first choice, but did not always keep to the same one each night, nor did he seem able to make up his mind which to choose. Monocle would perch on a tree and watch while he flitted from one box to another, poking his head inside them, but not entering. Finally, she would get impatient and try to secure a roost for herself. Directly she flew to her choice of roosting-box, Baldhead pushed himself in front of her, preventing her entrance with a noisy scolding. She flew away but appeared to have chosen for him, for he entered that box and she chose another. (Great Tits do not roost together usually, even when they are inseparable during the day.) I think this was a bedtime game, as I have often seen birds behaving playfully just before going to roost. When nesting time comes round again Baldhead will let his mate have first choice over everything she wants, but in autumn and winter the male always takes precedence — with species that keep together all the year round. I have noticed there comes a time of change-over between the precedency, when both mates hesitate in a polite manner, apparently waiting for each other to have first helping of food.

In personal intercourse with Baldhead I am sometimes outwitted. His favourite food is nuts and last autumn I brought some indoors in a paper bag, giving him one which he ate on the rungs under a chair. Knowing he would tear open the bag to help himself to another, I wrapped it in a double-folded teacloth, rolling this round the bag and turning both ends under securely in a way that seemed impossible for a small bird to undo. I placed this on a side-table. I had my back to Baldhead while wrapping the bag and he could not possibly have seen what I was doing from where he was, under the chair seat. He soon flew to my hand for more nut, but I gave him cheese – his second choice of food. He threw this away with an impatient toss and looked up at me expectantly. Again I offered him cheese. He made a curious sort of grimace with his beak half-opened, refused to take the cheese and flew round the room, looking for but unable to find the paper bag. I left the room for a few minutes; on my return he flew out of the fan-light window with the haste habitual to him after theft. Several nuts were rolling on the side-table. He had pulled the cloth undone and torn open the paper bag, helping himself to a nut. I had never before wrapped food in this cloth or in any other kind of cloth, nor had I ever put bird food on that side-table, which was used for painting mater-ials, so he had no reason to suspect the cloth contained the paper bag, which was solidly covered with a double layer of cloth.

Baldhead also loves butter but knows he must not steal it from a plate and never attempts this unless given permission, as long as I am in the room. (Birds are so sensitive that they learn at once what is for-bidden and what is allowed, although they have no conscience over disobeying when one's back is turned!) But in cold weather, when butter is hard and spreads nobbily, he flies up and snatches knobs off the bread with pick-pocket deftness, just as I am about to put it into my mouth. As he is encouraged to feed from my hand it would be unreasonable to scold him for this, but perhaps to be on the safe side, he always flies quickly out of the window with this spoil, instead of eating it indoors, as with food given him.

Baldhead, like many other Great Tits, soon finds out the correct way to open small boxes in which I keep tit-bits for birds. Instead of just hammering in an attempt to open, he carefully inspects any new type of box, the construction apparently being noted; he then tries to open it the right way, generally succeeding after a struggle unless it is too difficult for me to open easily myself. Match-boxes are held by the feet and pulled open by the beak; if the box is too stiff to pull wide open it is taken up, turned over and shaken to get out the bits. A tin lozenge box, hinged one side, on first being used, was examined all over with great care, then prised upwards, attempts never being made to lift the lid on the hinged side. The trouble with this box was that if he only opened it half-way the lid fell back before he could grab the food, but after some false attempts he got it farther open and quickly inserted his head before it shut. Sometimes he held it open with a foot. These are just a few examples of Baldhead's intelligence. Some Great Tits, equally at home in my cottage, never get beyond hammering on lids although they have had the advantage of seeing other clever ones opening the boxes. Intelligence varies a great deal within the species.

3

One of Jane's offspring by her first mate was another exceptional bird, who had the peculiarity of being unable to lay eggs. She was one of three females reared from a first brood. Her two sisters were attached to each other and always together, but this odd one seemed afraid of other birds and was always alone. When they came near her she flew away with a little squeak, then began nervously examining her toes. She had very small feet, this perhaps partly accounting for her fear, feet being used for defensive purposes. While still a fledgling she had some crown feathers plucked; afterwards she shunned other birds more than ever, but sought my company, spending much time on the rails underneath my chair. At night she roosted on the picture-rail above my bed, being the first of many Great Tits to do this. When her crown feathers grew again they had a ruffled look which earned her the name of Curley and like other of my birds, she soon responded to her name.

Like her parents, Curley had much individuality; I could never mistake her for others of her species even as a fledgling, and her manner sometimes suggested self-consciousness. When other birds crowded round me at feeding time she would disappear; when all had gone she stealthily approached me from behind, climbed up the back of my calves and nipped me gently underneath the knee, then flew to a perch opposite me, alternately examining her toes and throwing me quick glances. Directly I called her name she came eagerly to feed from my hand. This nipping developed into a game which was frequently played. When she saw me engrossed in some quiet occupation, she stole up behind me and gave a gentle nip in some unexpected place, or else hopped all over me, hunting for the most threadbare part in my clothes; when found she carefully parted the threads into a convenient hole through which to nip me, always looking up at my face afterwards as if to see the effect. This game continued until I gave an agonised squeal, and then I saw the light of contentment in her eyes as she perched opposite, alternately glancing at me and examining her toes.

If Curley was hungry and had failed to make me realise the fact, she either flew to the window-curtains and plucked out the velvet pile or tore at the pages of the telephone directory, eyeing me with an expectant expression all the while for she knew such destruction always attracted my attention and was not allowed.

Her adult plumage was sleeker and brighter than other female Great Tits, but in other respects she was decidedly female, both in appearance and in her ways. Her first mate was a fine-looking bird of the large type – Great Tits varying much in size. Curley gave him trouble, being slow over decisions always. He worked hard, trying to get her to decide upon a nesting site, but for several weeks she wavered between the choice of four nesting-boxes in my orchard, each box having to be defended from other eager Tits by her bold, determined mate. She would work hard at enlarging the entrance hole of one box, then look inside, give a little squeak, as if of fright, then fly away to another box. Her mate followed her, giving encouragement and persuasion by continually entering the boxes himself and calling to her from inside in nestling-cry imitations. All Great Tits do this but the female generally spends more time inside prospective nesting-holes and boxes than the male; also, she calls to him in the same nestling-cry sounds.* Curley popped in and out of each box hurriedly and silently, except for an occasional nervous sounding squeak before flying to the next box.

This indecision continued until all neighbouring Tits had hatched their young, then Curley's mate grew very restive and they both left my garden for a month. Curley reappeared afterwards alone and idled about in the trees, sunbathing and taking life easily. Her plumage was in excellent condition, and I was sure she had not brooded eggs while away.

The following year much the same nesting behaviour occurred but with a different mate. She had no young, was absent from the garden

---

* This nestling-cry imitation has been mentioned previously and is quite different from the fledgling-cry adopted by the female when she wants her mate to feed her.

for three weeks, returning with her crown feathers plucked, probably by her exasperated mate for he had shown much impatience before they left the orchard.

The third year she chose for her mate a queer, nervous bird with two large, horny whiskers that crossed over his beak, making it difficult for him to grip food. He was excessively nervous and excitable and when taking food from my hand, he usually dropped it in a flurry of agitation as he flew away. 'Whiskers' was untidy looking, his movements flustered and jerky, but he was a faithful bird and had reared his brood alone the previous year, his mate having died soon after the young were hatched.

Curley was now in beautifully sleek, bright spring plumage and she had gradually overcome fear of other birds. She stood up for herself and even took the initiative in small disputes. Judging from continual observation of both birds during winter and early spring they had paired with no courting display, just before nesting-time. This year Curley chose the largest and best-looking nesting-box in my garden without indecision and Whiskers, having strong feet and an alarming looking beak, appeared to defend the site by bluff and sudden nervous flurryings to and fro in front of the tree where the nesting-box was hung. Curley became brave in defence of this nesting site, her small feet seeming equal in strength to one or two larger females with whom she came to grips. So between them they kept the attractive and coveted nesting-box.

But the progress of nest-building was extremely slow. Curley gave the impression of playing at nesting. Whiskers, like her former mates, spent much time coaxing her to hasten building – so it seemed – by loud furores of cries like a chorus of nestlings, both from inside and outside the box, but Curley only occasionally made a little sound from the nesting-box and she never responded to Whiskers' display. Every morning she took a little moss to the nest, and between each lot there was a long interval spent in tearing bark from an apple-tree twig above her nest. Whiskers began to show impatience, continually chasing her, for he wanted coition, but she dodged away from him – I think, never allowing it.

Birds were very early over nesting that year (1946); on May 26th other Great Tits' young were fledged, while Curley still was bringing the few bits of moss each morning; every time, before going to collect more, she plucked leaves from a sweet-briar that grew by her nest and tore them into shreds, throwing down the pieces. There was so much impatience of manner in these destructive attacks that undoubtedly they were caused by frustration over her inability to produce eggs. From that date Whiskers began to lose interest in the nest and Curley was without his attendance for most of the day. She still vigorously defended her nest, and on May 28th Jane's fledglings were driven from her territory with much angry noise. By May 31st she had collected enough moss for the nest but it was not lined or neatly finished. She slept in it each night and every morning popped in and out several times, but no more nesting material was brought. Much of her day was spent twig-biting and plucking sweet-briar leaves more impatiently than ever. Whiskers sometimes appeared when Curley was absent. Her appetite had for some time been very poor, although she seemed quite well and looked in perfect condition. For the next fortnight either she or occasionally her mate kept guard over the empty nest, but they were never there together. He was more flurried than ever, snatched food from me spasmodically and generally dropped it as he flew away.

On June 14th I found an old Partridge's egg in a field and placed it in Curley's nest. She at once began to brood it, and although Whiskers had not been there when I put the egg in the box or near Curley before she began brooding, within one minute he arrived on the scene in a flurry of excitement, a caterpillar dangling from his queer beak. Curley put her head out of the nesting-hole to receive it and both birds seemed happy at last. How did Whiskers know she was sitting? He could not have known through sight or sound; he had never fed her before nor had she ever made the fledgling-cry sound that female's utter when ready for their mates to feed them; they had not even been seen together in my garden for two weeks, yet without having seen the egg or been near when she entered the nest to begin brooding, he came hurrying across my neighbour's garden with a caterpillar directly she brooded the egg. In his enthusiasm, he brought her food every few minutes that morning and Curley, instead of being intent on sitting, kept putting her head out of the entrance hole to watch for his arrival. In the afternoon she left the nest for three hours, much disconcerting her mate who arrived at the nest with caterpillars and seemed puzzled not to find her sitting. He flew round the garden, calling her in gentle tones; not finding her, he kept guard over the nest until her return, when he enthusiastically fed her again.

The next day she only sat half the morning and during that time was fed attentively; as before she did not sit closely, and frequently put her head out of the entrance hole. The following fortnight she played at brooding the large egg for an hour each morning, Whiskers entering into the spirit of the game by feeding her while she was sitting, then they separated for the rest of the day, taking turns at guarding the nest or leaving the garden. Curley's mate never offered her food off the nest as is usual when affairs are normal. I noticed her appetite suddenly became very hearty after the arrival of the Partridge's egg.

From July 1st to 6th both birds were often away; they always returned singly. Curley now made no attempt to brood, although she still guarded her nest noisily from other birds' proximity. She had grown fatter and looked in fine condition while all other females, exhausted from the labour of rearing families, were thin and bedraggled.

From July 6th to 31st Curley was seldom seen in the garden; she never entered her nest. Whiskers rarely appeared, when he did it was only to snatch food nervously and disappear again. As in former years Curley returned permanently in August, idled her time away in sunbathing and her old habits of examining her toes and playing nipping games with me. Whiskers did not return with her. Curley's moult affected her appearance much less than other Tits, as in previous years.

During autumn she again scolded any bird that went near her nest and she roosted in it at night. On warm October days she took a little more moss to the nesting-box which I have never seen other Great Tits do in autumn. Whiskers returned in October for spasmodic snatchings of food from me, which he generally dropped while hurrying away. In early winter he disappeared altogether.

One night at the end of December, poor Curley was killed by a neighbour's cat, her remains being found beside her nesting-box, which the cat had pulled to the ground after severing the thick rope that had fastened it to the tree.

4

Curley's two sisters, although inseparable as fledglings, parted company in autumn. One left the garden altogether – or was killed without my knowledge – the other, an especially intelligent bird, I always had under close observation. She was named Twist, because her tail had a peculiar twist from roosting with it pressed sideways. After her moult it was straight but gradually became more and more curved until it was sickle-shaped and ragged.

Twist always appeared to understand some things that I said to her and, unlike other birds, she seemed to enjoy being caressed when young. Like all Jane's offspring, she never had the least fear of me; when a full-grown fledgling she took naps perched on my knee or preened her feathers while on my hand or shoulder. I could raise my hand, with her on it, close to my face and gently rub my cheek down her back. She would turn up her face and look into my eyes, but never moved away while I continued the caress. Birds generally dislike being touched on the back, although they do not mind gentle stroking of breast feathers or downy sides. I think this is because parent birds sometimes stand on the back of their young to push them from an exposed perch if a Hawk flies overhead, also, when the young are full-grown and demanding food too roughly, the parent will occasionally subdue them by standing on their backs.

One day when I was caressing Twist in this way I said: 'Give me a kiss.' To my astonishment she quickly touched my nose with her beak – a bird's kiss. I thought her response was chance, but the next day she again responded to these words in the same way, and she continued to do so for the rest of her life. If I asked her a second time running she looked at me with a puzzled expression without responding, and if I repeated it, to try and coax her, she looked at me very crossly. But when an hour or two's interval had elapsed she was again responsive. When hungry, if she saw I had cheese for her she would often give three hurried kisses in succession, but even if I had cheese to coax her, she would not kiss if asked twice running. She never offered one without being asked, and other words did not produce a kiss.

Birds have different ways of asking for food. Twist always perched on my shoulder and looked up into my face with a pleading expression. If I said, 'Have none,' her expression altered, she looked annoyed, left my shoulder and perched opposite me with a fixed stare. If I said, 'Shall I get some?' she instantly flew to the door, her expression eager and expectant. While I went to the kitchen to fetch cheese, she either waited on top of the sitting-room door or followed me, and with head craned forward, watched for the cheese she knew I was getting for her.

She would only eat cheese or nuts; if offered bread or fat she looked at it a moment then picked it up and chucked it across the room, looking up at me afterwards with her pleading expression. If I gave her another piece of food that she disliked she swung round sharply on my hand so that her back was towards the food. She then turned round again and looked up at me, clearly expecting this time I should understand she wanted cheese or nuts. I did understand and this time she got what she wanted, but I did not encourage her to chuck food across the room by giving her cheese when she did this.

Many of my Great Tits are remarkably clever in finding out where food is kept, but Twist was particularly sharp. She had only to see once where I kept her favourite food and she remembered. I have seen her trying to push a saucer off a plate because, while waiting on the kitchen door for me to get her cheese the previous day, she saw me place a saucer over what remained on the plate.

Twist's mate was a bird from a copse over the fields opposite. He had an unusual variation of the 'Tee-chu' song:

This was sung very fast and repeated over and over again with wonderfully vital rhythm.

Twist, not her mate, chose her first nesting site. She fought hard to keep in my garden, but the pugnacious Tits drove her off and the nearest site available was in a vent pipe by some farm buildings over the road. When her young were nearly ready to fly she came in to roost on the picture rails above my bed. One evening she went to her roost earlier than usual. Three of her young had flown, the others were still in the nest. She looked dreadfully exhausted, and dispensing with her usual preening preliminaries, straightway settled down to sleep, her head tucked under her wing. But a minute later she stood alert upon her perch, head craned forward; next moment she had flown out of the window and over the road to her fledglings, apparently just for one more look to make sure all was well. In another moment she returned, this time not stirring until dawn, when, as usual, she flew over the top of drawn curtains and through the fanlight window.

The following evening she looked more fagged than ever. Her nine young had now flown and this is always the hardest day for a mother Tit with a large brood. That night Twist's exhaustion made her oversleep. She did not waken until I drew back the curtains at seven-thirty (D.S. time). Instantly she realised it was late and started up with an anxious expression; uttering a loud scolding-note, she flew hurriedly over the road to her fledglings. Never again did she sleep indoors. This was an interesting use of the scold-note; perhaps she was annoyed with herself or else feared harm had come to her neglected young.

The following two years Twist nested in her mate's copse over the fields, perhaps because the vent pipe had been removed and her mate favoured his little wood as suitable territory. When the white violets showed their bloom in the copse, Twist's visits to my cottage began to grow shorter and less frequent. By the time the bluebells were in full glory she was very hurried on her occasional visits, for there was an ash-tree in the copse with a neatly chiselled hole in its stem and now the interior of this hole had become the centre of Twist's thoughts. When cowslips covered the meadows her visits to my cottage ceased while she reared her young. With birds the time of nesting affairs is more correctly reckoned by the flowers in bloom than by calendar dates.

As I often walked to the copse it was easy to keep in touch with Twist, who came with her mate to my call. Sometimes she flew to meet me over the cowslip meadows before I called; perched on my shoulder, she ate the cheese I brought while her mate fed from my hand.

When nesting days were over Twist came back to my garden for many long visits each day and spent much time indoors with me during autumn and winter. Unlike her mother Jane, who was inseparable from her first mate, Twist generally came alone, her mate seeming to prefer the copse while she preferred my garden – the home where she was born. But I noticed sometimes when she was indoors she suddenly stood rigid, with a tense expression, and dropping food she was eating tucked between her toes, she hurriedly flew out of the window and across the meadows towards the copse. Occasionally she paused a moment on a tree outside the window, still with a tense expression, before hurrying off to her mate – for I sometimes followed her and found she flew to him. The sudden tension of her body and her facial expression, as if vision was centred inwards, her eyes not focusing upon what was in front of them, suggested she was responding to some form of communication from her mate. Perhaps her sensitive ears, through windows almost closed, could hear his call from far away across the meadows, his distant voice, tuned to her ears, piercing the louder intervening sounds of road traffic or tractors. Or had she and her mate some other vibrant or telepathic form of communication? Other cases of communication without sound or sight, such as Whiskers knowing Curley was at last brooding an egg, although he had not been near when I placed it in the nesting-box, nor within sight of Curley, who had kept completely silent, may point to the latter conclusion. Curley had been in her nest every morning on previous days, yet he never once fed her. How did he know the egg was there unless Curley had communicated this to him by some telepathic means?

In Twist's fourth winter her tail became more bent and ragged than ever from the heavy snows. In the intense cold of early February, 1947, she died, frozen in her sleep, five weeks after her sister Curley.

Curley and Twist had never been friendly towards each other and they always reacted in the same way when meeting in my room. Twist would fly into the crook of my arm and look very surly, while Curley flew to the top of a window curtain-rod. If Twist stayed with me for more than a few minutes, the velvet pile of the curtains suffered, for Curley began to tear it out and though I shouted at her she would not stop this destruction until I went towards her, Twist then flying away out of another window. Then Curley perched opposite me and examined her toes with her self-conscious air, and when I called her name, flew to my hand for food. They were both on good terms with Jane — their mother — and all other Great Tits, even the non-residents who only came to my garden and indoors during winter.

5

The following year, 1948, was Baldhead's third nesting season. He and Monocle brought off their first brood successfully, and a week after their young were fledged he became restlessly interested in nesting-holes again. His mate showed little enthusiasm for a second brood, but Baldhead's vigorous displaying over nesting-boxes eventually brought response, and she began to build another nest in a different box from

her first. When the young were hatched Baldhead was far more attentive in looking after them than his mate. She took much time off,
feeding and resting in the trees while he devoted himself to nursery
duties, scarcely stopping to take food and never resting in daytime. At
night he slept in a roost on the picture-rail above my bed.

Another pair of Great Tits, Puggy and her second mate, also had a
second brood, a week older than Baldhead's, her nest being in the
front garden. Here the position was reversed; Puggy was the attentive
parent. She and her first mate were the Pugnacious Tits. They had
been a very devoted couple – both first-year birds when mated. Perhaps Puggy was not naturally pugnacious but had adopted her mate's
dominant and aggressive ways towards other Tits for when he died
and she mated a peace-loving bird, who never fought, she became
timid and nervous in her manner to other birds. After her mate died,
watching her subdued ways it seemed she missed the spirit of the Pugnacious Tit. Although nesting in the same hole, she and her second
mate allowed other birds to bring their young anywhere in their territory unmolested. But he did not show much affection for her. She
often put her head out of her nesting-hole, expecting him with food
when she was sitting; he rarely came, compared with her first mate.
Nor did he show enthusiasm for feeding his young. She was always a
devoted mother and for eight years had reared two broods. Perhaps
Baldhead had inherited some of his nesting enthusiasm from her for
she was his mother.

On June 24th Puggy's young of the second brood were fledged, all
leaving the nest in an orderly manner, one after another taking flight
without hesitation. They were well-developed fledglings with quite
long tails, as Puggy never encouraged her young to early flight; she
liked them to be strong on the wing. Some parent Great Tits try and
coax them to fly when four or five days younger. The brood, on their
first morning, were taken out of my garden into the playing fields for
a few hours; in the afternoon they trooped back home, Puggy leading
them along with the charmingly gentle language that parent Great
Tits use. At roost hour she shepherded them into the oak tree that
grows by my bedroom window, and there they spent their first night.
Her mate took only a small share in looking after the family, a few
days later he deserted them altogether and hid in bushes, resting himself while she did all the work.

On June 25th Baldhead's young flew, three or four days before their time. They were very small and weak on the wing. Their mother deserted them for an hour at a time, but Baldhead was a wonderful father to the brood; by degrees he coaxed them to safe perches in my orchard hedge, where he attentively supplied them with food all day long. On July 2nd his mate stopped feeding them altogether, but he continued until July 8th. Only two out of seven had survived; these were charming fledglings called Teaser and Buffer, henceforth much in my company.

In contrast to Baldhead's mate, Puggy was then still attentively feeding her four surviving young, although they were older by a few days. Even on July 13th she was occasionally supplying them with food and calling them to her in gentle tones for caterpillar hunts around the bushes. That day Baldhead's fledglings were feeding from my hand when she wanted cheese for her young. She perched on my wrist and, through a half-opened beak, hissed at them. They ignored her and went on feeding. But she was really very tolerant of all young-sters, and the hiss was never repeated when she stopped feeding her own. On that same day I have this note of Baldhead's behaviour to Puggy's young.

July 13th. Baldhead looks annoyed if fledglings are feeding from my hand when he wants food for himself. There is not room for him to get at the cheese on my palm when Puggy's four youngsters are sur-rounding it, so he perches on my arm and makes complaining squeaks with a little display which no one heeds. He then hops to my shoulder and pecks sharply at my cheek. I call out 'don't,' and he walks round the back of my neck, fussily tweaking me and pulling my hair; he then returns to my hand, stretching out his head and pushing aside the fledglings, in turn gives each one a light tap on the head. They still do not leave my hand, so I give Baldhead cheese on my other hand.

Both Puggy and Baldhead look ragged and worn in plumage while the inattentive mates are both in good condition and later, during moult, they do not suffer nearly as much as the others.

On January 9th of the next year I recorded the following:

Great Tits suddenly begin disputing in hottest form, male fighting male; female attacking female. The dispute is over Baldhead's roosting-box, which he has occupied since autumn and during last winter. It is hung to a tree by my window on the right side of cottage and is in

Baldhead's orchard territory. At midday I see him and his rival rolling on the floor, feet interlocked, and throw a match-box to frighten them apart. They fly out of the window, one in hot pursuit of the other. Half an hour later a lamed, ill-looking Great Tit flies in through the fanlight, landing in a gasping condition plop on my lap, unable to stand. At first I do not recognise Baldhead, so different does he look, his eyes dim with pain, feathers fluffed out and head bowed over his chest so the frontal markings are not seen. Every now and then he flinches, his body heaves with each breath. He is too bad to eat properly, but I get a little cheese into him as he lies there. Other Tits enter the room, he seems unconscious of them until suddenly, although I hear nothing and no bird enters the room, he cocks his eyes, an alertness of expression just visible through the look of pain; next moment he has flown into a corner and lies hidden behind a shoe against a wardrobe. Then his victor enters the room. This bird is very strong, powerful and dominant. He is called Inkey because of very black, wide frontal markings. He was not bred in my garden and only appeared last autumn; Baldhead, brave in defence of his roosting-box, has been defeated by this outsider; if he recovers he has lost his territory, owned all his life – for the orchard territory includes this side of my cottage.

January 10th. Baldhead is very ill, his eyes are clouded and he is still unable to stand on either leg. He flies in at the fanlight and flops on to my lap several times a day, choosing a moment when no other birds are in the room. If Inkey enters after him he quickly hides on the floor behind furniture but I am generally able to prevent Inkey's entrance by closing all windows directly Baldhead appears. He understands the safety of this, and if in hiding, immediately I close the windows he flies from cover and lies on my hand to feed. I keep him on my lap for as long as possible, but the other birds flying around the windows, trying to get in and tapping furiously at the panes, makes Baldhead restless; after a time I open the fanlight and he flies away to the trees. Other Great Tits never molest him in his weak condition. Inkey is sometimes outside when he flies away through the fanlight, but there is no chasing of the defeated by the conqueror.

After a week or two Baldhead began to improve. By February 7th he was able to use one leg quite normally, but the other usually hung down behind him when he perched. Since losing his old roost in his territory he had slept every night in a box hung to a tree on the other side of my cottage. But now all Great Tits began displaying over nesting sites so Baldhead had to hold his new box in his weak condition. It was interesting to find that although his rivals could easily have ousted him by brute force, they seemed to regulate methods of warfare to those of which he was capable, so he held his ground for some weeks. He worked very hard, displaying in many original ways and inventing much odd language, the trick of his fledgling days also coming into use again, for I sometimes saw him hanging to a twig upside down by one foot, swinging the lame leg in the air (page 16). Sometimes he would flop on to my lap, panting with exhaustion after his efforts, but as soon as he had a little recovered he flew out again to hold his nesting site. His mate, Monocle, had been very retiring since Baldhead's injury; she shunned the presence of other Great Tits but came indoors to feed a few times daily.

Baldhead, after struggles to keep his territory

On March 29th, Puggy started building in her usual tree-hole, the same side of my cottage as Baldhead's new box but about thirty yards distant. The oak tree where her fledglings had roosted last year stretched its branches over Baldhead's box. The next two days Baldhead only appeared in my garden three times to take food, his mate completely disappeared. On March 31st Puggy's mate chased Baldhead away from the left side of my cottage into Inkey's territory, on the right. I saw Inkey pursuing him up the orchard. A little while later Bald-head flew into the cottage, landing flop on the floor at my feet. He was breathing heavily, with feathers fluffed out, his crown feathers were plucked, the right side of his face was bare and a slight trickle of blood showed near his ear. At first I was afraid he was dying, but after a few minutes he took food and water which revived him; in ten minutes he was asking me to open the window – closed to keep others away – and although he looked a wreck with his featherless head and lame leg, his spirit was undaunted; he would yet hold his own over entrance to my garden and cottage.

He did not appear again that morning. I grew anxious, but after a search, found him with his mate in a large oak tree just beyond the top – or north – side of my orchard. He perched on my shoulder to eat cheese, then began flying around the oak with his mate, evidently searching for a nesting-hole, but there was nothing suitable. I fetched a nesting-box, first fixing it on the back of my orchard hedge too near the border of Inkey's territory. Baldhead showed great excitement when seeing the box but turned to me with a scold-note at watching where I fixed it and flew to the other side of the oak tree. I moved the box to his chosen spot, then he eagerly entered it, with the usual nestling-cry sounds. His mate gazed through the entrance hole, then grew fidgety, for she wanted him to come out so that she could try it for herself. She hopped restlessly from twig to twig outside, began pulling bark from a branch and hammering it with her beak, but Bald-head would not stir. Eventually she went inside with him, then both came out together, inspected the box all round and afterwards took turns at entering – Baldhead always staying inside the longest. They showed obvious delight at having this box; she began building that afternoon while Baldhead limped around, chasing any Tits who went near the box. I left food and water near their nest, but next morning Baldhead came to my cottage several times, choosing a passage along the back of the orchard hedge to avoid arousing Inkey's anger again by flying near his nest. Now Baldhead had begun nesting away from Inkey's or Puggy's territory no objection was made to his passing the front of the cottage and entering to get food whenever he liked, but his mate never ventured to enter my garden until her young were hatched.

Inkey and Baldhead spent hours displaying together over the boundary between their territory at the top of my orchard while their mates were building and sitting. It was interesting to note that the strong male never took advantage of his opponent's physical weakness in these disputes over boundary. Baldhead limped about, defending his rights by various methods of display, and now, for the first time this year he sang the 'tee-chu' song from tree-tops, in a voice rather feeble and cracked, but in a manner full of confidence and spirit. Although he looked a complete wreck with his featherless face and head he was livelier than at any time since his first defeat; his appetite increased and his leg strengthened a little, although he will always limp. The lamed leg appears to have been dislocated – it is not in normal position when he stands. He and Monocle reared their brood successfully, but this year he did not attempt a second for he was too exhausted. After his moult he looked beautiful again in new plumage and was perfectly well except for his limp.

Inkey's mate, called Smoke, had chosen to nest in a large petrol tin instead of the nesting-box taken from Baldhead, and now an interesting case of territorial behaviour occurred in connection with this box. A pair of Great Tits, who were complete strangers to my garden, surreptitiously took this nesting-box, which was in Inkey's territory while keeping a territory of their own beyond Puggy's, over the road. This they flew to straight from the nest, without ever perching in Inkey's territory except upon the nesting-box. While Smoke was busy putting finishing touches to her nest, the stranger female crept in silently from over the road, flying behind bushes and entering the box with her moss, then returning for more material, always collected from over the road in her land, although my garden was rich in moss. At first Inkey was so engrossed with Baldhead at the top of the orchard that he may not have noticed these stealthy strangers, but a few days after they took the box I saw Inkey peering inside with an expression of interest. To my surprise, he made no objection to these silent strangers, who never uttered a note or displayed when he went near their nest or looked inside the box. Not once did Inkey chase the strangers or display over boundary lines as he did half the day with Baldhead. There *were* no boundary lines, for the strangers made no claim to land, they never fed in my garden, even at the bird-table; all they wanted was the nesting-box, for they had no suitable hole in their territory over the road.

When their young were hatched, all food was fetched from their land, carried along the border of Puggy's into Inkey's territory to their nest. When Inkey's young flew they often perched on the strangers' nesting-box or the tree branch above and were fed by their parents, the strangers never making the usual protest at having chattering fledglings on top of their nest while the nestlings inside were only just hatched. They could not protest, for it was Inkey's land and his offspring had the right to perch on their nesting-box. If either of the strangers was in the nest when the Inkey family were surrounding it it stayed inside the box until the territory owners moved away. Their nestlings were very silent for Tits, the atmosphere in which they were reared perhaps subduing them, for my other Great Tit nestlings call out in chorus at entry of their parents and after they leave, the strength of their voices increasing every day. The strangers' brood began to fly two weeks later than Inkey's young, the former at an earlier age by four or five days. Only two flew the first day, these the father bird took straight across the road, for the first time perching on trees in my garden while coaxing his babies to follow him. Meanwhile, the mother bird looked after the rest of the brood. They flew two days later, and were quickly taken over the road by their mother. Inkey watched these young make their first flights with an expression of great interest and hovered near the nest, restlessly although not interfering, until all had gone. It seemed he had allowed these Tits to use the box under some understanding that no claim was made to land outside the box, and their young must be taken away directly they flew. Or perhaps it was because these silent strangers behaved as they did that they were never interfered with by Inkey and Smoke, who were both very dominant with all other Great Tits who entered their land.

In all other cases in my garden of stranger Great Tits trying to nest in boxes on territory belonging to other couples, they have been forced to abandon their half-built nests, but in these cases they used a small part of land surrounding their box.

When the silent brood had disappeared from my garden it was interesting to find that the parents, particularly the mother bird, often returned to fetch food for the young from inside my cottage and from the bird-table, which they had never done while using the nesting-box. All my Tits having been fledged two or three weeks before may have partly accounted for this, for strictness of territorial behaviour was then relaxed, but all the while these strangers were nesting I had seven pairs of Great Tits entering the cottage for food which they took to their young although their nests were not all in my garden, Puggy and Inkey being the only ones that owned territory surrounding my cottage. My Tits allow entry to be made to the cottage for food by those accustomed to using the rooms for the winter season. But the strangers did not risk entry while they were using the nesting-box within two feet of one of my windows, I think, for fear of being chased away from their nest if the residents objected. The very day their young had left my garden the parents returned to fetch food; they ran no risk then of being chased from their young.

NESTING NOTES, 1950

January 29th to February 11th. All the autumn and winter Baldhead roosted in his favourite box, taken from him last year by Inkey after the battle that cost him a permanent leg injury. Now these two Tits are again disputing for the box and surrounding territory. Inkey is big and strong, Baldhead is now physically weakened but his spirit is still indomitable. For a week he displays from morning till night in many original ways, the most prominent invention being a succession of flying leaps, two or three feet high, over Inkey while keeping in stiffened display pose and uttering many strange notes. Inkey merely struts along the ground in an elongated pose, head up, tail spread, wings drooped, while Baldhead leaps over him. Inkey then flies to the coveted box, Baldhead rushes at him, putting phenomenal speed into the charge and Inkey retires; B. repeating the ferocious charge. He has grown a spike on the tip of his upper mandible which makes his beak look very long and gives him an impressive appearance. Sometimes I see him lying on the window-ledge near the box, looking utterly exhausted and a queer strained expression on his face. But he holds his ground by incessant effort and vigorous display, hardly pausing to eat the food I give him – he chucks it away half-eaten.

Since the summer a grey-type female with a white star on her crown has followed him about persistently. His old mate, Monocle, never seeks his company. She had not enough vitality for Baldhead and had grown lazy over feeding their young. This new female, called Star, is full of life and she takes her share in fighting for the territory. Often she comes to grips with Smoke – Inkey's mate – and as they roll together on the ground, feet interlocked, Baldhead hovers over them, in agitation squeaking out high-pitched notes. His lamed leg was gained through this form of combat; he wants to separate the females, but is not always successful. They do not hurt each other and seem equally matched in strength. By February 15th Inkey and Smoke were ousted from Baldhead's territory. This year he has kept all his head feathers intact. His battle had been won without coming to grips with his opponent. He spent the next two days resting on a tree near the boundary of his land on Inkey's side. He now ate all the food given him with much eagerness and each night he retired very early to roost in the hard-earned box. He had been an early rooster since his lameness, for he gets tired sooner than other birds.

February 18th. Baldhead's new mate, Star, enters his roosting-box at 8 a.m., stays there a long while then enters another box nearby. On February 20th he as usual goes to his roost in good time, but he quickly flies away, showing signs of excitement, flicking his tail and wings, then breaking into song. From every tree-top in his land he sings, announcing his news to the neighbourhood – for his mate has chosen her nesting-box, and for the first time is roosting in it. He then returns to his box and looks through the entrance hole at his mate. He tries to enter but she turns him out of his roost, for Great Tits do not usually sleep together, and females often dislike their mates in their nesting-box (possibly a habit that has grown through having frequently to use narrow holes where space is very cramped, and there is need to keep the nest free of excreta). Baldhead shows agitation and insists upon entering his box, but soon reappears through the entrance hole, looking flustered and hen-pecked. He takes a turn round his territory then tries again with the same result. He impatiently hammers at the entrance hole, flies round the garden and tries once more. After he enters, there is a sound of fluttering wings inside the box and he emerges, looking very cross. This continues for an hour. All other Tits, who roost later than he does, are in bed, the Blackbirds seek their roosting perches, dusk is giving way to night, but Baldhead is still trying to get into his roost. He has tried dozens of times, always his mate forces him to beat a hasty retreat and he gets more and more fussed and worried, but will not give way. He goes through many frustration antics, consisting of restless movements, twig hammering, tearing leaves, etc., and gives whimpering cries, then at last, almost in starlight, he enters and remains in the box. All is quiet inside the roost.

February 23rd. Each night the same struggle at roost hour, although she gives in a little sooner, perhaps too sleepy to resist any longer. I placed another box, of similar make, just above the old one. Baldhead tried it but soon came out and persevered with his mate over the favourite box.

February 28th. The problem continues but B. is gradually winning. Last night, when Star thrust him out for the seventh time he flitted around the roost uttering long volleys of excited scold-notes. She jumped up and down inside the box, trying to catch glimpses of him without showing her face outside the entrance hole. He stopped scolding, flew to the box, intending to enter, but loud rapping noises came from inside, this driving him away. More scold-notes ensued. The new mate of the Robin Dobs, a sprightly young female, flew at Baldhead, gave him a peck on his rump and flitted hastily back to her roosting tree. This suggested, 'shut up!' He soon made a successful entry and all was quiet.

March 10th. Baldhead has gradually overcome his roosting difficulties. Star now lets him enter without any fuss.

March 24th. She begins taking moss into the box. All goes well with Baldhead at bedtime.

Baldhead's efforts of continuous display with Inkey had left him slightly lamer than before so he did not make much protest when some other nesting-boxes in his territory were taken by stranger Great Tits. The result was that altogether nine pairs nested in my garden. Besides this, Teaser, a Baldhead offspring, came to me with her young – she had always nested in the orchard next door. One day I counted sixty Great Tits in my trees and hedges. I could distinguish the different broods by their voices and details of utterance in their fledgling calls, for each family, when newly flown, had some characteristic feature in the call or cry, either of tone quality, pitch, details of rhythmic utterance or speed of repetition of the notes which constitute the fledgling call. In some of the broods there were one or two members that had distinctive calls of their own from the very first. As the fledglings grew the call gradually altered a little and then each bird's voice developed some degree of individuality. The parent Great Tits always knew the calls of their own young and there was never confusion over the feeding of these many broods. Each family of young kept together remarkably well and when occasionally a fledgling found itself among the young of another brood it first tried to get food from the stranger parents by crying and fluttering its wings; finding this unsuccessful, it called loudly and turned its head this way and that, to listen for the sound of its own family, and when the familiar notes of its own brothers and sisters were heard, it quickly joined them, never flying towards one of the other broods, who were calling from another part of the garden. Only once I saw Baldhead feed a small fledgling that was not his own, but directly after he had given the caterpillar he looked at the baby with a queer, surprised expression then gave it a gentle tap on the head which sent it flying to its own family nearby.

There is a good deal of variation in the shades of colouring among Great Tit fledglings, some having white cheeks, for instance, and some yellow, the latter being altogether more golden in hue in the parts where the former are whitish.

Naturally, there was a difference in the dates that the broods were fledged.

1. On May 28th Monocle's seven young flew. They were hatched on May 8th, so were all well-developed fledglings with fairly long tails. She took them away from my garden for several days to a hedgerow that was much haunted by Magpies. When she returned only three had survived. Monocle, Bald-head's former mate, had paired with a younger male and their nest was in orchard territory adjoining Bald-head's. Monocle kept away from their territory boundary and avoided contact with Star or Baldhead; she seemed very nervous of them. The two males frequently entered each other's territory when seeking food, the owner always displayed mildly but did not forbid entrance.

2. On June 3rd the Silent Strangers of last year brought off their brood from a nesting-box by my gate. As before, they took their family over the road, were very quiet in all their nesting affairs and their young very subdued in voice.

3. On June 4th the Back Wall Strangers' eight young flew, in very

orderly manner, one after another all flying to the same trees and shepherded to the back of my orchard hedge, away from Baldhead's nest. They had nested in a box tied to the back or north wall of my cottage — Baldhead's box being on the west side — and all their food had been sought from trees north of my orchard. They avoided contact with any of my resident Great Tits.

4. On June 4th Baldhead's ten young flew. Hatching began on May 18th. (Further details later.)

5. The same day two members from the Front Wall Strangers' brood were fledged. The remainder flew on June 8th. These strangers were so surreptitious that until they began feeding their young I never noticed that the box, hung under cover of japonica against the front wall of the cottage, was occupied. I had seen the male displaying with Puggy's mate outside the french window, but thought this stranger was the mate of a female called Tiptoe.

6. On June 11th Tiptoe's young flew. She was a gentle female who had been with me for a year. When she first came she was unable to use one leg; it healed with the foot a little twisted so she was unable to grip with it. Her mate was a newcomer who always kept in the background. Their nesting-box was on the apple tree by my west fence, so he sought all his food in the neighbouring garden. Tiptoe, perhaps because of her lameness, fed her young chiefly with food taken from me, after the first few days of hatching. The father bird supplied all natural food. Baldhead and Star made no objection to her presence although she frequently went near their nest, which was close to hers but hidden by an intervening macrocarpus tree. I think this tolerance was because of Tiptoe's weak leg, for I notice that Great Tits are usually tolerant of birds that are slightly hurt or lamed. Tiptoe kept her brood always in my garden, generally on the west side. The seven young used sometimes to perch on me while she fed them and when she stopped feeding them they followed Baldhead's brood indoors to take food from me. It was amusing to watch them all trooping in through the fanlight with much chatter. The members of each brood always kept together.

7. On June 11th Dimple's young flew. She and her mate nested the far side of my north hedge in the orchard. She had trouble with Monocle, whose territory adjoined hers, when she brought her brood to me. Dimple persisted although it cost her the loss of many feathers in disputes.

8. On June 14th Smoke's young were fledged. She had nested secretively, later than the others, in a nesting-box hidden among foliage in my east hedge in the orchard. Most of her nest-building was done in the evenings, when other Great Tits of my garden were taking time off to bathe and preen alongside the playing-field hedge, where there is a small brook. She worked very hard while at it, but took longer than the other females to build her nest because she dared not work if they were nearby. Inkey always kept the far side of the hedge, to avoid contact with the other males. By the time Smoke's young were fledged Monocle was no longer feeding hers and Baldhead and his mate too busy with their brood to notice Smoke, who had free run of the garden and orchard for the three young which she kept with her. Inkey took the rest of her brood away with him, and I have not yet seen him again.

Teaser and her mate, Timpano, adopted rather the same method of separation, although it is not usual with Great Tits. Teaser brought four of the young to my garden and Timpano reared the others in the neighbouring garden and beyond, in the playing fields. Teaser flew over to Timpano sometimes but he never came here; Baldhead and Puggy's mate objected to his presence in my garden. I sometimes took my Tit-box to the playing fields to give Timpano cheese for his young, then Teaser, who no doubt saw me from a tree-top in my garden, used to hurry towards us, her four fledglings following after her. She then took turns with Timpano in flying down from the trees to get cheese from my Tit-box for her young.

9. June 18th. Cross and his new mate brought off their young, who were hatched on May 30th. This bird was Puggy's second mate. His ways were peaceful while she was alive, but his next mate did not give him an easy time and, evidently through frustration at her lack of response, he became bad tempered towards other Great Tits, so was given the name Cross. On March 24th Puggy had started to build her nest in her mate's roosting-box outside the east window of my bedroom. Ten days later she disappeared and probably had become the victim of a cat, for the previous day I had twice chased one who was stealthily watching her collect moss for her nest. She was ten years old and had recently become less alert and her movements slower. Her nest was almost complete. Unlike some other female Great Tits she had made no resistance to her mate's entry into her nest at bedtime and so he slept with her after she started to build in his roosting-box. After

Cross lost Puggy he made many entries to the nest during the day, but he now would not roost in it and slept down a gutter pipe nearby.

Cross's new mate was an old-looking bird with no sheen on her plumage. She was nervous in manners and a complete stranger, who somehow knew that Cross needed a mate. She turned up within two days. The mystery is how it comes about that a bird suddenly appears when a vacancy arises for a new mate. After Puggy's disappearance Cross had continued to sing from exposed positions in his territory in the manner usual to Great Tits who are nesting and exactly the same way as he had sung when Puggy was alive and building her nest. So how did this stranger know he now needed a new mate? Cross evidently wanted her to behave like Puggy, but she was very different. He expected her to take on the ready-made nest and did all he could to persuade her to enter, but she would not do so. For a fortnight he spent much of the day hovering over the nest, making nestling-cry sounds from inside and outside the box, trying to get his new mate to take interest in Puggy's nest, but after watching him for a moment she would fly away to the trees. Sometimes he fetched a caterpillar, called her to him then held it out to her, but before she could take it he flew to the nesting-box, turned round to see that she was watching, gave another call-note, then entered the box and quickly put out his head through the entrance hole, showing her the food, and again withdrawing into the nest; he repeated this several times, all the while giving excited little call-notes. She never showed the least sign of response and always flew away, leaving him inside the box. He made distressed cries when he found she had gone and, dropping the caterpillar, he went after her. He became fidgety and restless; he would not eat, the food he took from me he chucked away after taking one bite. During this fortnight she spent much time at the window, clinging to the frame and looking at her reflection in the glass. Sometimes she displayed at it a little, being the only Great or Blue Tit among my many residents and strangers that has done this: nor have I ever found other Great or Blue Tits take any notice of their reflections in mirrors. On the first time of seeing the reflection they usually look behind the mirror, after this they appear satisfied and no more interest is taken in the reflections. Cross's mate evidently was puzzled and twisted her head into every possible position while examining the reflection and often tapping the glass. When she found this noise attracted my attention she tapped for purposes of getting food. As soon as she started nesting, the window-pane ceased to interest her.

After a fortnight she began to build in another box I had put up close to Puggy's, but until she brooded her eggs she slept in a little roost fixed close to my east window. This worried Cross, for most females roost in their nest after starting to build, if not sooner. Every evening he tried to coax her into her nesting-box by making baby-cries and flying backwards and forwards from her roost to the nest, but as usual she was unresponsive, so he tried to enter beside her in her chosen bed. This she would not allow. He then restlessly flitted around, giving odd call-notes every few moments, first looking inside Puggy's nesting-box then inside his new mate's nest. This always went on for half an hour after she had gone to roost; finally, he began calling her in very gentle tones then flew to her roost and peered in at her, but she spread her wings in protest against his entering. Again he visited both nests then at last popped down the gutter pipe to bed. When she began sitting he slept in her small roost by my window. He had become fidgety and was by then bad tempered with all other Great Tits except his mate. He looked very off colour and bedraggled as if beginning to moult prematurely, but his restlessness ceased after his mate began to sit. She has never come into the cottage through the fanlight like the other Tits and seems dull-witted, compared to them, in many ways. She feeds from my hand out of doors or just inside the french window.

Her young were only sixteen days old when they flew. Monocle's were three weeks old when fledged and Baldhead's three weeks all but one day. The ages when Great Tit broods leave the nest show much variation. The three mentioned above had exactly the same type nesting-boxes, with entrance holes the same height from the nests. I have watched some parents push their young back into the nest with gentle scold-notes if they try to fly a little before the parent thinks fit.

Baldhead's brood of ten all flew on the same day, although they varied much in size. Some of the bigger ones were more nervous of the plunge than the smaller ones. I watched them leave the nest, some in the morning, others at different intervals during the afternoon. First came two well-grown male fledglings, who made strong flights to the trees. The third to appear at the entrance hole was the smallest of the family. Her behaviour differed from the others, instead of looking around at the trees and distant objects within her view she kept her eyes fixed on the ground and for five minutes gazed at the earth beneath her while her larger brothers and sisters jumped about inside the nesting-box, impatiently awaiting their chance for exit. At last she spread her wings and half-floated, half-fell to the ground on the spot that she had stared at so intently. She was odd looking, with a completely bald forehead but a thick crop of feathers that rose to a peak on her crown. Her wide baby beak nearly reached to her bright eyes. As she scurried along the ground on legs that looked very long in proportion to her tiny body she looked so like a queer goblin that she became Gobline – the 'e' to denote her sex. She tried to hide in a clump of flowers while her mother called her from above, trying to coax her upwards to a safe perch, but Gobline was not yet able to fly. I put out my hand, intending to assist her to a branch, but she turned round with an indignant air, hissed at me loudly and snapped her beak many times in defiance. As she wished no interference I let her alone; she then ran into cover of long grass beneath a tree.

The rest of the brood flew at different intervals of the day, to safe tree-perches. At roost hour the parents showed much concern over Gobline, for she could not fly to the bushy tree where the others had been safely settled for the night on thin twigs and branches where no cat could climb. Gobline slept on the ground, the tall grasses and wild flowers surrounding her. I was careful not to walk near so that no trodden pathway should help cats to discover her. Next morning she was alive, vigorously calling for food. She still could not fly, but by aid of little fluttering leaps she managed to perch on a low fork of a cow parsley branch, a foot above ground, looking more goblinish than ever in this raised seat among the flowers. I guarded her carefully so that no Magpies or Daws should seize her in this rather exposed perch. Her second night was again spent hidden in long grass, but the following day she was able to fly to the trees. Her forehead was now covered with feathers, but the peaked crown still remained. Her quaint ways and appearance were fascinating to watch. She was still very tiny compared to all the other Great Tit fledglings in the garden, in fact I have never seen one so small that survived. She had a big appetite for natural food but disliked cheese and spat it out. Baldhead and Star remembered this when feeding her, and it was very rarely that they took her artificial food, although the others of the brood were by now having much cheese and bits of peanut given them – the peanut first nibbled by the parent to make it softer for the fledglings. Gobline was determined to get her fill of natural food, and she sat wing fanning and calling for attention until she had got more than her share. Often I saw Baldhead trying to stuff large moths down her throat; she liked moths, but even in the first days of being fledged, if given food that was too big to swallow easily, this precocious fledgling preferred to eat it in the grown-up Tit fashion, tucked between the toes. So these large moths always ended by being eaten in this way. Usually the young Tits do not learn to handle food between the toes until several days after they leave the nest. Long before the others she was finding moths for herself, hidden beneath low-growing plants in the flower-beds.

On June 11th, five days after the young flew, Baldhead's lame leg gave way again; how it happened I do not know, but it may have been through overstrain of the apparently dislocated joint. At seven-thirty that morning I noticed Star was rushing about in a rather hysterical manner, seizing food from me in much more haste than usual, but Baldhead did not appear for the next hour. Then he flew up, and flopped on to my lap, unable to stand. I held water before him and he drank thirstily, afterwards eating some cheese. He lay still for ten minutes, then Star flew to him and, in an excited manner, began displaying – quivering her wings and making nestling-cry sounds. Baldhead responded by a faint sound but lay still until she had flown to the young. A moment later he resumed work on his one leg. Although obviously in pain and often balancing by the aid of a spread wing for support, he struggled to stuff food down the fledglings' throats. He showed much courage, for he looked very ill and was not able to eat much himself for the next few days. Star stimulated him by displaying frequently with much wing fluttering; she worked far harder than before and took the main share of feeding the young while Baldhead took occasional intervals of rest that he so much needed. They never left my garden. Their brood was alternately kept in the front part or the orchard.

On the day that the parents ceased feeding their brood, Gobline also strained one leg and she could not get about to find food for herself. For several days she was dependent upon me, but I could not supply the natural diet that she liked. She developed an unusual cry that sounded like sobbing, whenever she saw either of her parents, but they did not give her food. Often Baldhead and Gobline were perched side by side, both holding up their game legs in exactly the same manner. She kept uttering her sobbing notes in his ear while her wings quivered slightly; Baldhead never repulsed her but he did not respond to her cries. I caught green flies and grasshoppers for her and also occasionally a few small spiders which she liked, but when I offered her a large black one she and all the other fledglings shrank in fear from it. The spider escaped across the room, to be devoured by an adult Great Tit with much relish, for this is one of their favourite foods. Gobline was still very undersized and now she had to spend her day either sleeping or remaining motionless, hunched on a perch. Two of her big brothers noticed this and often tried to urge her into movement by sidling towards her along the branch where she was perched and, with much chatter, giving her gentle pokes. She held her own, turning upon them in the same manner as she had once repulsed my effort to assist her to a safe perch. Her brothers drew back when she snapped her beak and hissed at them, but they soon came forward again to continue their teasing. They were very gentle with her and probably this enlivened her day so I never interfered with the big brothers' playful behaviour.

In a fortnight the leg had quite recovered. She had grown rather snappy towards all the other fledglings, probably as a result of the troubles she had encountered through her handicaps. This snappiness ceased after several days, during which time she grew quickly to the average size for a female.

Gobline never quite lost her sobbing note, which she later used in an abridged version when wanting something. She had for some time slept every night above my bed, alternating between two boxes, one round and one square, that the other Tits had not tried to occupy. But one evening at the end of July, another youngster Great Tit was in her round roost-box when she came to bed; she hesitated a moment, then hopped into the square box, apparently unperturbed, but the next second she flew out and, like a whirlwind, fluttered her wings over the entrance of the occupied box while making fierce pecks at the occupier until he came out and the two birds, with feet interlocked, rolled together on my bed. I called out, 'Stop it!' then both flew to the window-ledge, shaking their ruffled feathers and uttering scold-notes, which were taken up by several other birds, indoors and outdoors. For ten minutes Gobline and the male Tit she had attacked remained a few

feet apart on the window-sill, both looking up at the roost and apparently each waiting for the other to make a move. Finally, he flew to
the same roost again, then Gobline flew off, out of the window. A few
minutes later she returned to the window, glanced up at the roost,
gave a nervous squeak, shook her feathers and disappeared again. That
night she slept outside. The following evening the other Tit went
early to bed in another box, adjoining Gobline's two roosts. When she
came in a while later she appeared nervous of going to either box, perhaps not knowing whether the Tit was again in one of them. After
hesitating for several minutes, perched on the window curtain-rod,
she crept along the picture rails towards the roosts and quickly slith-
ered into the square box. She did not look to see whether her other
roost was occupied, and I fancy, if it had been, she would not have
made objection, for since that sudden outburst her behaviour had been
very meek and mild with other Tits. It is usual for Tits to keep their
own roost and try to expel others who occupy it, but I have not before
had a young Tit try to keep two roosts, although adults will keep
others from entering roosting-boxes in their territory.

The next evening the male again took Gobline's round box and she
crept along the picture rails to her square roost. No sooner was she
settled there than he stampeded out of his box, noisily giving warning
of an attack and when he spread wings in display at the entrance of
Gobline's square roost she remained quietly inside. Then he began to
try and turn her out by entering it. I said, 'Stop it!' He took no notice so
I stood on the bed and touched his tail. At once he left Gobline alone
and returned to the round box. For many nights afterwards the male
youngster occupied the round roost and Gobline the square one. She
always waited until he was in his bed before seeking hers.

Of other Great Tits under observation during ten years at Bird
Cottage, I noted the following: Knicky's first mate died after three
years. They had always been together, winter, autumn and summer,
perched upon the same bough or bush, calling to one another if
moving from tree to tree. They were single brooded and always nested
in the same hole. Knicky's second mate, Tapper, was not often with
her out of nesting season, but they nested in that same hole for two
seasons. Then Knicky died. Tapper always tapped at my french
window to attract my attention before he came indoors through the
fanlight to feed from my hand.

Snatch and his mate, called Grab, were two lively birds and inseparable mates, with character and appearance much alike. The male had narrow frontal markings which were more characteristic of a female. Both seemed always in a terrific hurry, they flew faster than most Great Tits and their movements were jerkier. They snatched food from me in a wild manner although not afraid, for they entered the room, but as if they had urgent appointments and must seize all the food possible in their only spare moment. When Grab died, Snatch chose a completely different sort of mate, who was quiet mannered, smaller in build and greyer in plumage – where other Tits are greenish. She was so tame with me that she would sit on my hand and pull strands from a ball of wool for her nesting material. She clung to my sleeve and called to me gently when I had not the wool in my hand which she wanted me to fetch. The next winter Snatch disappeared. He had never been very attentive to this mate. She chose Whiskers – he was later Curley's mate – for her second mate and died while the nestlings were tiny. Whiskers reared them with great difficulty and they obviously were not fed enough, but he did his best for the large brood. I think one of this grey female's offspring was Baldhead's mate called Grey, her appearance and ways were so very alike, and I find these small variations of colouring and size are often inherited, as well as gentleness, bold manners or other characteristics.

Another couple, especially devoted in their ways and very emotional over nesting affairs, brought disaster to their young by their enthusiasm. Their voluble excitement and displaying when rearing young was so noticeable that it attracted the attention of all their enemies, so their young came to grief. Three times they tried the same nesting-hole with failures, then left the garden and never returned. Their nesting-hole was afterwards occupied by the Pugnacious Tits who successfully reared two broods each year for many years, but their ways were completely different.

I have never found two females laying in the same nest. The average clutch has been nine with one egg often not hatching, or eight with all eggs hatching. Almost always every nestling is successfully fledged but about half of the brood usually fall victim to their enemies within two or three days of leaving the nest. Blue Tits have sometimes had twelve all hatching from one female, so probably most of the larger clutches that are seen occasionally are from one exceptionally prolific bird.

GREAT TITS

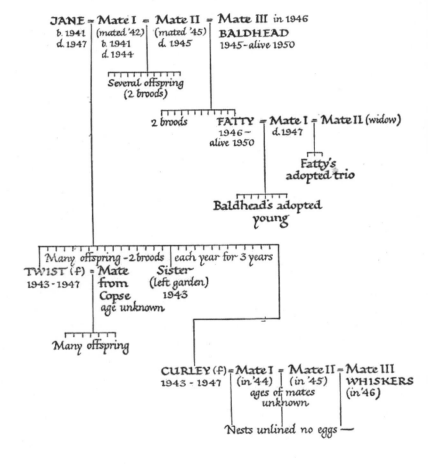

JANE = Mate I = Mate II = Mate III in 1946
b. 1941 | (mated '42) | (mated '45) | BALDHEAD
d. 1947 | b. 1941 | d. 1945 | 1945-alive 1950
        | d. 1944

Several offspring
(2 broods)

2 broods   FATTY = Mate I = Mate II (widow)
                1946 – d. 1947
                alive 1950

Fatty's
adopted trio

Baldhead's adopted
young

Many offspring – 2 broods │ each year for 3 years
TWIST (f) = Mate   Sister
1943 - 1947   from   (left garden)
              Copse   1943
          age unknown

Many offspring

CURLEY (f) = Mate I = Mate II = Mate III
1943 - 1947 │ (in '44) │ (in '45) │ WHISKERS
            ages of mates   (in '46)
               unknown

Nests unlined no eggs —

GENEALOGICAL TREE

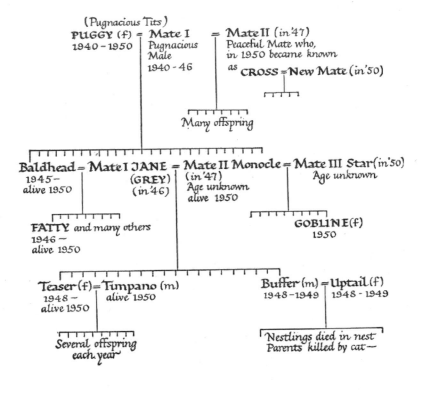

(Pugnacious Tits)

PUGGY (f) = **Mate I** = **Mate II** (in '47)
1940 – 1950 | Pugnacious | Peaceful Mate who,
| Male | in 1950 became known
| 1940 – 46 | as **CROSS** = **New Mate** (in '50)

Many offspring

Baldhead = **Mate I JANE** = **Mate II Monocle** = **Mate III Star** (in '50)
1945 – | (GREY) | (in '47) | Age unknown
alive 1950 | (in '46) | Age unknown
| alive 1950

FATTY and many others
1946 –
alive 1950

GOBLINE (f)
1950

Teaser (f) = **Timpano** (m)
1948 – | alive 1950
alive 1950

Buffer (m) = **Uptail** (f)
1948 – 1949 | 1948 – 1949

Several offspring
each year

Nestlings died in nest
Parents killed by cat —

(f) female
(m) male

CHAPTER 3

Bird Biography: Blackbirds

1

In part one of the previous chapter, when telling of the Pugnacious Tits' altered behaviour to Jane after her brood was fatherless, I mentioned that birds will adjust their territorial laws to meet circumstances. The following is another case in point.

One of my Blackbirds, during nesting season, strictly guarded his territory in my orchard from all neighbouring Blackbirds including one called Thief, from the next-door orchard. Because I mowed paths through the long grass of my orchard and threw scraps there for the birds, my Blackie had hard work to keep the others away, but he did while food was plentiful elsewhere. His mate was unlucky, an egg being taken from her clutch by a Rat or Daw. She deserted and built again, but the same thing happened. Thief's young were hatched and he made many attempts to steal scraps for them, but Blackie was vigilant and chased him off. When Blackie's mate started brooding her third clutch, Thief's mate was brooding her second. Owing to a drought, food now was scarce for Thrush tribes, the clay soil being hard as iron. Thief was finding it really hard to find enough for his three fledglings and then my Blackie, who had no young to feed, altered his territorial behaviour. Thief was allowed to come for the food but Blackie escorted him backwards and forwards each time, and always stood over him while he fed the fledglings.

Thief normally kept Blackie out of his territory so both had adjusted their behaviour to meet the circumstances. It was amusing to watch Blackie accompany Thief into his domain, wait beside him wherever he perched and, as soon as the young had been fed, the two would return for more food, Thief first and Blackie close on his heels. In a couple of days the three fledglings were following their father along my orchard paths, always with Blackie bringing up the rear. Each time Thief picked up food the fledglings clustered round him with open beaks and Blackie stood beside them, head tilted forward, his expression alert while he watched the food being swallowed by a fledgling. All other neighbouring Blackbirds were still refused entry into his territory – but I think their young were not fledged.

Then the drought ended, and with the softening of the soil came the hardening of Blackie's territorial defence. Thief and his family were chased off every time, but Blackie still had no young to feed. I have known many other cases of relaxation of territorial behaviour during drought, and in snow or prolonged frost. My Blackbirds normally are very strict over their boundary defences, perhaps more so than is usual because of the extreme popularity of my garden. The sensible discrimination over relaxation of this strictness seems to prove territorial behaviour is not wholly automatic, as some ornithologists maintain, but adjusted by minds with good reasoning power.

Thief's mate was an unusual bird with white edgings to her wings and tail, and a white star on her forehead. She was always very trim, with every feather in place and altogether a remarkably lovely bird. He was usually disgracefully untidy, with feathers looking as if never preened and his eyes had a battered look, the yellow rims being incomplete. She never appeared to have any of the usual intercourse with other Blackbirds, her decorative touch of albinism perhaps making her aloof and others avoid or respect her.

The ragged Thief well deserved his name. I never saw a Blackbird so sharp at thieving. In summer I had meals in the orchard while watching the birds. At lunchtime Thief would choose a perch in his orchard where he could overlook me and keep his sharp eye on my plate. If it contained meat he waited until my head was turned away to watch some bird behind me, then he swooped down silently but quick as lightning and, before I had realised what was happening, had snatched meat from the plate and flown off with a loud chuckle, my Blackbird in hot pursuit. The rapid pickpocket action of a really first-class bird-thief seems a gift which cannot be acquired; I find some Great Tits have this natural talent, others are always comparatively clumsy over their many attempts.

Even Thief's songs were stolen tunes, cribbed from neighbouring Blackbirds with little embellishment added – as is usual when one Blackbird copies from another. (See Bird Song, Chapter 11, pages 150 and 153.)

For six years Thief and his pretty mate reared their families next door in the same rambler bush. Then she died and he mated an ordinary female who carried on in that same bush. He died two years later.

One of Thief's offspring had some odd characteristics, and as this bird chose to include part of my front garden in his territory I have had him under close observation.

2

Thief's son did not gain his territory easily, for the old Blackbird, who owned all my front garden, was very tenacious.

While the old bird was in moult he allowed many youngsters to feed on his lawn, among them Thief's son, still in fledgling attire. When autumn came the old Blackbird, in his new plumage, was vigorous and strict over possession. All the young ones left except Thief's offspring, who hung about at the far end of the lawn under cover of bushes and the hedge bordering the road. The tall apple-tree there was his favourite perch; here he preened himself and basked in the sun, also he sometimes sang a very quiet subsong, only audible quite close to the tree. He kept a watchful eye on the old Blackbird, seizing opportunities to trespass on the lawn for food or running up to the bird-table by my window when the old bird was occupied with other neighbours at the back of my cottage.

It was a mild winter and in January the youngster began efforts to gain half the front garden for nesting territory. With care this original bird selected a large oak-leaf from the many dead ones on the ground and, with this in his beak and head held up high so the stiff brown leaf was very conspicuous, he rushed to battle with the old Blackbird in the middle of his territory. There was a scrimmage in the flower-beds as they chased one another in and out of the bushes then flew up, beak to beak. Suddenly the youngster turned tail and ran quickly back to the far end of the lawn. Carefully he placed the oak leaf on the grass then rushed back to combat. The battle was long and fierce. The youngster came out of it looking battered but the old Blackbird, who was the first to give up, looked in perfect condition.

An hour or two later the youngster picked up the same oak-leaf and, brandishing it high with a confident air, strutted right across the old Blackbird's territory. They fought less fiercely than before, much being the usual Blackbird walking chase, backwards and forwards and in and out of the bushes, the youngster brandishing his oak-leaf with a cocky air. Occasionally they flew up beak to beak, and after a little the young bird retired to change his war-worn oak-leaf for a fresh one, again running to attack with neck stretched high, the stiff brown leaf prominently held in his upraised bill.

For many days the two Blackbirds fought, always the youngster with his oak-leaf, like a talisman, held in his bill. Once he tried carrying several oak-leaves, but found they hampered him and soon put them down, selecting one large, stiff leaf. He never chose any other kind of leaf although there were many on the ground. At the end of a month Oakleaf, as he was now called, was a battered-looking bird, but he had won half the lawn. He now turned much attention to song and nesting affairs.

Oakleaf's originality again was shown in song, for he made a more effective use of vibrato than I have ever heard before. His phrase was

superbly sung, and the tone of his long-held final note with the impassioned vibrato compelled concentrated listening and much thought about the soul of a bird. Perched high on the tall old apple-tree, this odd-looking, battle-scarred Blackbird sang by the hour, perfecting a variety of original tunes. Unlike his father, he never copied a phrase from another Blackbird, but went on composing his own melodies, embellishing them, turning them all ways and experimenting in different tone effects, tempo and pitches.

Nesting days began and one fledgling was reared from his first brood. Although the old Blackbird also was feeding his young, Oakleaf often encroached on his territory, unearthed a worm and held it up high, as if swaggering before his old enemy. Their battles went on and before Oakleaf's mate hatched her second brood the old Blackbird had died of wounds inflicted by the strong beak of the impetuous young battle-scarred bird. He was now grotesque looking, with the feathers all plucked from his crown and bare patches above his eyes.

Up to the first week in August, Oakleaf continued to sing, but his mate failed to rear any young from their second or third broods. Perhaps his exceptional powers of song attracted attention of enemies to their nest. The rest of August Oakleaf spent much time squatting on the lawn, his bald head upturned with his beak pointing to the sky and a dazed expression in his eyes. Unlike most Blackbirds, he did not hide among bushes or trees during moult, but posed like a scarecrow in a prominent position, apparently to keep away others from his hard-earned land.

On September 4th, in the early hours of a wild, windy morning, Oakleaf was absent from the garden, and I saw a young Blackbird with adult plumage not yet complete performing a very unusual dance on his lawn. She chose a sheltered strip, surrounded by flower-beds, with a rose pergola behind. Lifting her wings high so the pale undersides were seen, she flickered them rapidly and gave a little leap into the air, then darted forward a few paces on the ground and, with more quick wing flickers, turned sharply round, darting, leaping and turning again, with occasional light wing-flicking. Every movement was at lightning speed and full of airy grace. Suddenly she stopped and pecked the lawn vigorously, scattering small clods of clay soil. Snatching one, she threw it with a sharp twist of her head, darted after it, seized it again and threw it as if playing a rapid game with a ball. Again she made a springing leap, and flicking high-raised wings at intervals, she whirled round three times in a circle of a few feet, keeping to the ground but with motion too rapid to know if she was running, hopping or propelled forwards by the curious wing-flicks. Suddenly she stopped, her body sunk on the ground, her head upturned.

It was the most surprising performance, for the dancer's movements were not typical of a Blackbird. To the bird-watcher, this exuberant dance was in keeping with the spirit of the wild, south-west wind. In a moment she rose again, stretched upwards her wings for the flicker, gave one springing leap and repeated a quick circling spin, as if bouncing round aided by occasional wing-flicks. Then she stood still with lowered head, as if intent on looking for food, and another young Blackbird, son of Oakleaf, flew up to her and began pecking the earth. For a moment the two birds stood back to back and vigorously pecked the ground, then the dancer sprinted across the lawn and flew up to one end of the pergola. Oakleafson followed and flew to the other end. But the dancer turned her back to him and in an absorbed-looking manner, plucked leaves from the rambler and chucked them down, while young Oakleafson slowly hopped towards her. Suddenly the dancer turned and with one quick wing-flickered hop, she landed the other side of him. For a while they stayed back to back, still as effigies, then the dancer flew to the lawn and again began her graceful, wild dance, this time watched by Oakleafson from above.

Once more the two young Blackbirds stood back to back on the lawn, Oakleafson vigorously pecking the earth, the dancer turning dead leaves over and over as if absent-mindedly. Suddenly she flew rapidly to a tree, he following a moment afterwards.

Later in the day she again flew to the lawn. Oakleafson watched her from behind the pergola as she began her light wing-flicker and leap, but this time the grotesque-looking Oakleaf appeared, a drab creature with bald head and body dwarf-shaped with no tail, yet still possessor of a strong yellow beak. At sight of this queer-looking bird the dancer hastily disappeared. Perhaps she knew Oakleaf with his golden bill had slain her father two months ago, after many battles waged with an oak-leaf held in his bill.

So this remnant of a Blackbird strutted slowly up and down the lawn alone, proud possessor of the land perhaps, but with no spirit left to enjoy. In the background remained Oakleafson, for whose sake all the battles had been fought. He, too, now feared this battle-scarred bird of original ways and great power of song.

3

Oakleaf's behaviour was quite different in his second year. In October another Blackbird of his age, who had nested in my orchard, took possession of the old Blackbird's territory and Oakleaf gave up half his lawn to this bird without fighting. They appeared to settle matters by mild, friendly games around the new boundary of Oakleaf's territory, a flower-bed jutting out as a sort of no-man's land. The new bird, called Darky because he sang into the dark after other Blackbirds were asleep, would walk towards Oakleaf, who hastily picked up a piece of apple from under the tree and stalked round the flower-bed, holding the apple high, with head upraised and tail outspread like a fan. Darky rushed at him, he eluded the attack, dodged round the bushes and deposited the apple in Darky's territory just beyond the flower-bed. Darky ran after him, also with spread tail, upraised head and stiffly poised body. He pretended to grab the apple, but let Oakleaf intercept. Then the two birds paraded after each other in comically affected-looking attitudes, in and out of the flower-beds. They returned to the apple, which Oakleaf snatched and held erect cockily in front of Darky, who chased him back to his side of the boundary, where he dropped the apple and pretended to eat it. Darky dashed at him and they flew up together, snapping at the air playfully, so it seemed. Then the game began again as before. They spent many hours over it in October and November, apparently enjoying it and never suffering even a ruffled feather from their intercourse.

In January Oakleaf started running away from all Blackbirds, especially Darky, who frequently chased his flying form, for Oakleaf hurried off at first sight of Darky even if he was on Oakleaf's territory. In February (the year was 1947), during the prolonged snow Oakleaf seized food from my window-sill every day and when Darky protested he held the food high, quivered his wings, dramatically in effect, and spread his tail. This performance stopped Darky's protest, but Oakleaf always hurried away after eating and never appeared on the lawn until March 23rd. That day he crouched under a may-tree the far corner of the lawn, in his typical attitude, body low on the ground and head upturned, beak pointing to the sky. Suddenly his mate appeared and simultaneously Oakleaf disappeared over the hedge into my neighbour's garden. This was now the main part of his territory, but he still owned the corner of my lawn under the may-tree and a narrow strip of lawn behind the pergola, culminating in the apple-tree – his old song-perch.

The next day he again crouched motionless under the may-tree, his back towards his mate who pretended to feed behind the tree. Then she flew right up to my window in Darky's land, Oakleaf immediately following in curious looping flight, with an original high-pitched chuckle. He alighted behind her. She turned rapidly, jumped over him and flew back to the may-tree, he following. Then Darky appeared, running up in a consequential manner and standing nearby with flared tail and cocked-up head, rudely staring at the lovers. Oakleaf was too engrossed in his mate to notice, so Darky returned leisurely to his own land.

On March 26th, Oakleaf paid a return visit to Darky, armed with a beakload of leaves and a long strip of paper dangling from his high-held bill to the ground. This load hampered his progress and he kept tripping on the paper-end, but his slow advance had a humorous, mock-triumphant air. He appeared to be enjoying himself immensely, his manner and expression being quite different from when he attacked the old Blackbird to gain territory. Darky ran forward and they flew up together in the flower-bed, but Oakleaf found his beakload tiresome. He flew back to his may-tree, carefully deposited the leaves and paper under the tree, then came forward again, but Darky meanwhile had flown back to my window-sill to feed. When he saw Oakleaf advance he ran towards him, Oakleaf hurriedly picked up two leaves and rushed to meet him. Beak to beak they flew up several times, posturing in between, then Oakleaf returned to his may-tree and placed the leaves on the ground, afterwards wiping his beak on the turf, opening and shutting his mandibles in a queer way, as if the taste of the leaves had been unpleasant. He and Darky had no more encounters.

That spring Darky sang better and more continuously than any other Blackbird but failed to rear any young. Oakleaf, who had failure the previous year, now reared all his broods, but had very little song. His voice appeared to have cracked; when he tried his old tunes there was no beauty in his feeble tones. This, and other cases, seems to show that song is detrimental to nesting. Also, this year Oakleaf was a more devoted parent. He often brooded the nestlings himself, even when they were nearly ready to fly, which I have not found usual with male Blackbirds. This extra precaution was no doubt to protect the young from marauders. The nest was in the same hedge as before, but when Oakleaf attempted to sing he chose a perch farther away from the nest. This sobered and sensible bird had also this year kept all his feathers intact.

Birds learn from their mistakes, quickly gaining wisdom from experience, which surely shows that their actions are guided by reason, not merely instinctive and automatic.

Oakleaf, in his third year, reinforced the oak-leaf with a stick which he brandished high as he ran to meet Darky in their boundary disputes. In his fourth year this original bird had yet another brilliant idea. He added a peculiar flight attack; when Darky approached his territory he seized his weapons, including the stick, ran to meet him and when close, put on a sudden spurt that ended in circular flight at terrific speed just above and round his charging opponent's head, landing again about two feet away from him, then running quickly back into his own territory and turning round to repeat this attack, which bewildered Darky until he got used to it. The flight charge was exceedingly clever, for hampered with leaf and stick, Oakleaf had found the usual beak-to-beak encounter unsatisfactory, he had to drop his weapons when they flew upwards with clashing bills. But his new swift flight finish gave no chance for beak encounter. Darky rushed forward on the ground to meet him, charging empty space while Oakleaf, with his weapons, did his quickly rounded aerial finish to the attack. Eventually, Darky took to dodging round bushes when Oakleaf began flight attacks, the bushes hampering this modern method of warfare and favouring the old-fashioned stalking chases. When Oakleaf's fifth nesting season arrives perhaps he will invent yet another surprise for Darky, as there seems no end to the originality of this Blackbird.

CHAPTER 4

Autumn Robin Notes

The autumn of 1946 preceeded an exceptionally hard winter. There was an unusual influx of Robins to my garden in September, battling for possession of a winter territory that would include the bird-table or part of my cottage. The following extracts from my autumn notes were written while watching the Robins or directly afterwards. It was interesting to find that my Robin, named Dobs, acted differently to each intruder. Dobs was in his second year.

August 26th. Dobs is now in bright new plumage, his manner is defiant and he seems equal to tackling anything. He has greedily taken both sides of my cottage, not leaving his mate the east half as he did last year. She has retired next door, to East Garden and has not appeared in mine for some days. Two new Robins are trying to advance from the west and south-west. They are antagonistic to each other as well as to Dobs. These two Robins are rarely seen, but from cover of the tall macrocarpus tree near the west wall of my cottage, one bird shoots menacing notes at Dobs, who warbles back quietly but threateningly and bristles all over until he looks enormously big. The other new Robin is attacking from south-west, by my garden gate. From cover of trees she shouts loud, hard, spasmodic notes, occasionally flying to the ground to pick up something, then hurrying away with 'tic, tic, ticks' before Dobs has time to attack. My garden 'ticks' all day long.

August 27th. Dobs's mate walks across the lawn with her head held high and mincing steps – the slim, long-legged female again. Dobs appears and she retreats slowly, now assuming a heavier figure, with shortened legs and rotund body. Muttering something under her breath, she retires to her next-door territory. Dobs warbles very quietly to himself – or her – from the hedge which separates the two territories. He keeps stretching up his head, alert to the possibility of repetition of his mate's boldness – sauciness better describes it! West Robin threatens fresh attack; fierce notes come from behind

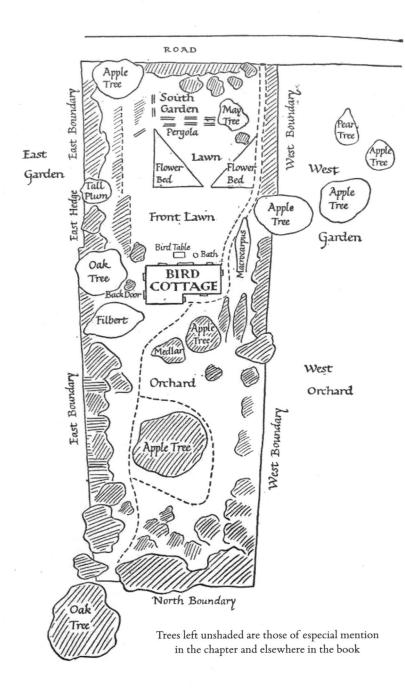

ROAD

East Garden

East Boundary

Apple Tree

South Garden

May Tree

Pergola

Lawn

Flower Bed

Flower Bed

Tall Plum

East Hedge

Front Lawn

Bird Table

o Bath

Macrocarpus

West Boundary

Pear Tree

Apple Tree

Apple Tree

West Garden

Apple Tree

Oak Tree

BIRD COTTAGE

Back Door

Filbert

Apple Tree

Medlar

Orchard

West Orchard

East Boundary

Apple Tree

West Boundary

Oak Tree

North Boundary

Trees left unshaded are those of especial mention
in the chapter and elsewhere in the book

Coming through the fanlight. A Blue Tit and Great Tits, hesitant because a huge camera is focussed upon them. *September 1950*.

Great Tits and the script! The bird in flight has just left my hand. *July 1950*.

Two youngster Great Tits, aged four months. *September 1950.*

A Blue Tit family.

Offspring of Baldhead on my hand. Age nine weeks. *July 1950*.

Great Tits in flight.

Opening a matchbox. *July 1950.*

Great Tit tearing a telephone directory. *July 1950.*

Interest in art! (The actual sketch is reproduced in the text because it is distorted through being photographed on a slant.) *July 1950.*

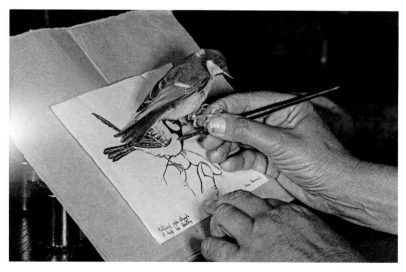

A youngster about the same age as the inquisitive one (above), but very different in character and appearance. *July 1950.*

Often Tits, several at a time, hop on my back when I stoop. The youngster below is an offspring of Cross. *July 1950.*

Robin at nest.

After a bathe. An adult Great Tit, in moult, taken by the bird-bath. *July 1950*.

A toy Parakeet fascinates the youngster Great Tits, but their first approach is usually cautious. *September 1950.*

A favourite toy of the Great Tits, which they attack vigorously then pull out the stuffing. *September 1950.*

macrocarpus tree. Dobs settles with him quietly but firmly in Robin language.

August 28th. Dobs is on bird-table with his mate, apparently friendly. He takes food from my hand, she picks up crumbs that are dropped. She seems a little nervous but Dobs is all smiles this morning, and no scolding ensues.

August 30th, and until September 4th. Dobs always comes alone, his mate not visible. Afternoon of 4th he chases her along their boundary hedge.

September 4th to 8th. Trouble with west Robin increases. Continuous flow of language from Dobs, and shouts from west Robin in the macrocarpus tree. Sometimes they roll together under the tree with locked feet but do not hurt each other. Dobs's language is superbly controlled; west Robin's hysterical sounding, spasmodic shouts do not seem nearly so convincing as Dobs's steady flow of language, sometimes uttered under his breath but sounding full of threatening meaning. In the early morning Dobs sings a beautiful song, but he can also sing in very different language when occasion demands. A Robin's song is more expressive in autumn than in spring. It has many more moods, sounding to me like fierce, threatening, coaxing, relieved, content, triumphant, morbid, conceited, wistful, determined, bored, hopeless – giving the impression his adversary is a fool and the world a hopeless affair! Garstang, in his book on bird song, called him the Chopin of bird music, but Chopin is frequently sentimental. Robins never are.

September 9th. South-west Robin has encroached towards Oakleaf's may-tree and the pergola. The south of garden is now her territory. She has little song and has the long-legged female appearance. She trips about very daintily. Dobs does not fight her, he is too busy keeping his mate from east side of cottage and west Robin from the west front of lawn. This afternoon Dobs has been singing from the top of east hedge plum-tree, a monotonous, loud song that sounds unlike his usual varied performance and seems just a noise to keep away the other Robins. He has grown very portly, weighs more than most Robins when on my hand, and his red breast is exceptionally brilliant, his mate pale in comparison.

September 12th. Dobs seems to have settled his territorial affairs to his satisfaction for the present, for he has been singing sweetly all day and has had no trouble with other Robins. West Robin sang a little from the macrocarpus, which is now apparently his territory boundary. Perhaps they are influenced by this fine, calm day – the first without wind for many weeks. Yesterday a party of Long-tailed Tits, perched on the wires alongside the road, had their tails blown backwards over their heads. They seemed nearly to lose balance. Today not even a high-perched Long-tailed Tit could have had the least trouble with his tail. Much of Dobs's day was spent perched low in the bushes, singing a continuous subsong which sounded like a long tale unfolding; sometimes while singing he half-closed his eyes and seemed unconscious of the world around him. How different his song and manner from that of previous days of dispute.

September 24th. Dobs is busy again over matters connected with his mate. South-west Robin and west Robin are sparring at each other by song and sighing notes, loud and hopeless sounding. Dobs pays no attention to them, he is concerned in keeping the back door, east side of cottage – which is the kitchen door – from his wife, who has been trying to edge her way into this crumby portion of territory. He is perched on the filbert-tree by the back door, his song quiet but ominous sounding, his eyes focused on his mate behind the tree, who retorts by loud 'tic, ticks.' With the loss of this door her last hopes of future crumbs would fail, but she is obviously afraid of coming too near Dobs; her strategy is a determined effort to take advantage of his need to defend the other side of the cottage. Every time his back is turned she edges slowly towards the back door, pretending to pick up food on the way, but not really eating or hunting for food. Her eye is always upon Dobs; if his attention is turned to her again she slowly retreats. He never attacks her and his song in dealing with her is always very quiet. He often pauses in these back door disputes to take food from my hand in the front garden, at the same time cocking his eye at west Robin, who sings much from the border of his territory. Sometimes Dobs perches opposite him for a few minutes to sing loudly, then he hurriedly flits back to the filbert-tree, for it seems he is particularly anxious to keep that kitchen door in his territory. His mate gives him more trouble than the two new Robins, perhaps because he is driving her from last winter's share of my garden and cottage front. But a fresh complication is developing from the west, for yet another Robin is pressing into west Robin's territory, from the sound of his voice, a strong male with much determination. West Robin is therefore tempted to try and encroach on Dobs, beyond the macrocarpus boundary. As the situation develops, Dobs leaves the back door and comes to deal with the other Robins, who fall into vulgar-sounding spluttering noises, as if losing their tempers. Dobs has a certain dignity about his methods of warfare. He uses strong language, but never resorts to mere vulgar splutterings or squeaking sounds.

A sudden silence from all the striving Robins while a party of Long-tailed Tits flit through the garden. It seemed the carefree atmosphere of this wandering flock affected the Robins, the breezy air of the Long-tails cooling the heat of the fiery Redbreasts' dispute. A sunny autumn day to these Tits means pleasant roaming along bright-coloured hedgerows, the rich spoil shared in friendly companionship, while to Robins such days seem to bring an urge for solitude, resulting in strife for sole possession of a strip of land where they can feed well in lonely retirement from others of their kind.

The Long-tails have passed by but their voices still ring from the distance, like many tiny, high-pitched electric bells. A long silence from the Robins, then Dobs begins to sing, three emphatic notes followed by one questioning upward scoop, which fritters away into rippling notes, the cadence four long, loud notes, dwelt on with increasing length and emphasis, sounding – anthropomorphically interpreted – as if that settled everything worth bothering about. The other Robins are silent except for a few desultory 'tic, ticks.' There is no more strife that afternoon. Dobs warbles quietly by my side, a gentleness in his character seeming reflected in this charming subsong.

September 26th. Dobs's song, to the accompaniment of pattering raindrops, is interrupted. The situation of west Robin is becoming serious. The new west-west Robin has encroached on west Robin and threatens to oust him from his territory. He has actually appeared beyond the macrocarpus on the lawn in front of the cottage in conflict with west Robin. Dobs, in fury, left his song-tree on East Hedge and, with feathers upstanding so that he looked enormous, flew at the two encroachers, sending them over the west fence. When he returned to his song-post his notes were long drawn and emphatic with one or two chuckle explosions interspersed. (The Robin has in his repertoire something similar to the Blackbird's well-known chuckle, although of course much higher pitched.)

Afternoon of same day. The two west Robins are again in conflict with each other under the macrocarpus-tree, but they chiefly sigh, squeak and shout, with much display and chasing. South-west Robin edges closer, seeming to wonder if she can gain ground from this new disturbance. She ventures nearer than ever before towards cottage on west side. Dobs gets annoyed and keeps flying down with ruffled feathers, singing from the ground near the macrocarpus – the west Robins' tree of dispute. But he dare not leave the East Hedge for long as his mate waits her opportunities from that side. It is a busy day for Dobs. He pauses a moment to drink from the bird-bath; between each sip he sings a spluttery phrase, sounding as if the water was bubbling in his mouth. He has to sing incessantly now, having to deal with four Robins.

Same Afternoon, 3.30. Yet another couple of Robins are pressing on west Robin and trying to get near the cottage via macrocarpus-tree and surrounding lawn. Four Robins are now disputing for this tree. From 3.30 until 5 p.m. a chase goes on, round and round the tree and its neighbouring apple-tree on the south-west. Dobs is furious; he sings incessantly with loud emphasis, often flying to the top of the bird-table to display, red-hot anger gleaming from his eyes. His head is enlarged, his body seems shrunken and his figure deformed. He is too agitated by this influx of Robins to take food offered him, he fears to stop singing or displaying for one moment, even to feed. South-west Robin is still trying to take advantage of west Robin's predicament; she now comes right to the flower-beds in Dobs's and west Robin's territory. Previously her boundary was Oakleaf's may-tree and the pergola adjoining. For many hours the flutter of Robin wings is heard, hitting against the leaves as they dash headlong in and out, round and through the trees. Dobs does not enter the chase, but sings continuously from the bird-table, with flashing eyes and alarming contortions of his usually attractive form; also, he now resorts to the splutter-note, which had not hitherto demeaned his song.

At 5 o'clock there was a plague of flying ants in my garden and probably high above, for the sky overhead was literally swarming with Martins and Swallows. Looking upwards, the masses of circling birds, crossing and recrossing each other at different levels, made a curious revolving motion so that one felt as if going round with them. As they circled higher and yet higher, seen far up in the heavens these hundreds of tiny specks looked like black snowflakes whirling upwards until almost lost to sight. Then a downwards motion began and a few swept close to earth, all gradually becoming visible as slender-winged birds with graceful, curving flight. Those that flew low looked surprisingly large – an illusion created by the smallness of others at higher levels. Again the masses of Swallows were wheeling upwards, forming innumerable gigantic patterns of intricate design, ever changing as they flew in rapid convolutions far into the sky above. Half an hour later this great migration assembly drifted eastwards, only leaving a small number hawking the flying ants at low levels over the garden. Willow-Warblers and Spotted Flycatchers also seemed enjoying the plague; even Sparrows were snapping them on the wing. When the Swallows had gone the plague increased still more and occasionally one of the four Robins paused in the chase to pick some from the trees or ground, but immediately it was pounced upon by another bird of the chase and dragged into the whirl round the trees again. Sometimes one Robin stood still to sing a phrase suggesting a Blackcap's cadence. His was no ordinary Robin song; perhaps he had lived away from his kind, with many Blackcaps around him. The others never stopped for real song, although there was much spluttering, squeaking or shouting of single notes and sometimes a long squealing note, ending in sighing sounds. During the evening Dobs entered the chase and when too hard pressed he resorted to something resembling a spit – excusable under the trying circumstances, for he had south-west Robin and his mate at the back door to cope with besides these four interlopers.

After dusk that night there were many agitated, defiant little Robin forms flitting about my lawn. The darkness gave them a chance to feed unmolested perhaps.

September 27th, 7 a.m. (*Summer Time*). The seven Robins are all busy again. Only Dobs has sung the Matins this morning. The rest began their day by 'ticks' and shouts that sounded like swear notes. The invasion of these new Robins is causing Dobs much uneasiness. The first new one, described previously as a strong-sounding male or as west-west Robin, has ousted west Robin from the macrocarpus and adjacent apple-tree and taken possession of the west front of lawn. This bird, in future called New Robin, is fiery and a match for Dobs.

September 27th (continued), 10 a.m. The glorious day of brilliant sunshine and clear blue sky seems to have made the Robins for a while forget their quarrels in a chorus of song expressive of the golden autumn morning. I notice, however, that Dobs sings louder than usual and without pause, as if wishing to hear only his own voice. His notes are also shriller than before the influx of Robins. He sounds at tension, but is singing well.

At 11 a.m. the chorus ceases and New Robin advances to the lawn on west front of cottage. He hops about jauntily, with bluff-swagger gait, on this new piece of ground, his eye cocked at Dobs on the bird-table, who glares angrily at him for a moment then flashes down to the lawn beside him, his body contorted, his head extended as if to bursting point and his language frightful. New Robin continues to hop jauntily, but keeps opening his beak wide to let out an amazingly loud and prolonged gutteral hiss, given with graduated intensity. As the hiss gathers vehemence the beak opens wider until the tongue is visible. His beak is scarcely closed again before this devastating performance is repeated, but he retreats slowly, so Dobs flies to his favourite song-perch, a tall plum-tree on East Hedge, commanding a good view of his mate's territory as well as being conspicuous to all the other Robins. He sings lustily until occasion demands another pounce on New Robin.

I am sitting close to the bird-table on the lawn. New Robin comes up to me and hints for food. Dobs shoots down from his high perch like a flashing meteor, in fury striking the intruder. They roll together on the lawn, feet interlocked, the grip of their clutching claws firm and evenly matched. At last one bird gets his beak at the other's throat. This seems a death struggle, so I separate the furious Redbreasts. But Dobs's blood is up, his flaming eyes match his fiery-coloured breast, and he at once attacks again. Loud hand-clapping at their ears frightens them apart. New Robin retires behind the macrocarpus-tree with a few desultory 'tic, ticks.' Dobs seems to think himself the victor, for he flattens his ruffled feathers and putting on his pleased expression, flies to his perch to sing sweetly, all shrillness gone from his voice.

September 28th. The Blackcap Robin is now singing from an apple-tree west of the macrocarpus. He has a mellow voice for a Robin, with Blackcap quality, and constantly repeats his phrase of a few notes resembling the Blackcap cadence. For ten minutes he sings this; it seems he has nothing else in his repertoire. Then come three low-muttered notes followed by long silence; New Robin is chasing him.

Dobs is singing from the back door filbert-tree, to keep his mate away. The four new invading Robins start 'ticking' and spluttering like a lot of alarm clocks. All are striving for possession of the apple-tree west of New Robin's macrocarpus and they start a swinging chase around and through the tree. Their flight is soft and silent, but as they dive in and out of the branches the flutter of their wings against the stiffening texture of autumn leaves makes a curious rattling sound. There now seems to be no anger in this chase, and I could believe it to be half-fun. If the Robins extend their chase to the pear-tree south of the apple-tree, the demure south-west Robin flies up, full of protest; this pear-tree is the border of her territory. The Blackcap Robin some-times pauses to sing his recurrent phrase, but any of the four that perch to sing are flown at and pushed into the chase again. For over an hour this game continues, if game it is. Then the four Robins all start sing-ing, the Blackcap Robin's mellow notes sounding like a tenor in a chorus of sopranos. Dobs flies to the front garden when the chorus begins, but this time, instead of singing shrilly, he warbles an exclu-sive, shimmering subsong, which stands out as definitely amongst the full-throated singers as one muted instrument does in a quartet of unmuted strings. At sundown the 'ticking' of all six Robins is heard at intervals. Dobs, who is used to having the bird-bath to himself at dusk for a lengthy splashing bathe, now finds it necessary to keep up breath-less 'tic, ticks' during a very hurried dip. From the way he keeps looking about him it appears he is nervous of other Robins interfering with his dusk-hour bath. After he has finished, New Robin occupies the bath for a long while.

September 30th. Robin-song rains down on me from every tree while I sit on the lawn. Blackcap Robin's song is now richer and includes more phrases imitative of a Blackcap. It is an unusual song, with few ordinary Robin passages. The south-west Robin has become more assertive for Blackcap Robin flew right across her territory and now seems trying to squeeze himself into a portion of her land. A long chase ensues on this southern part of the lawn.

I take my chair to the orchard, where I have not sat for many weeks. A Blackbird is singing subsong there, and I want to listen. Directly I sit down, Dobs appears and perches on my knee. Then New Robin comes 'tick-ing' along, looking like an artificial clockwork toy bird, the way he jerks up his tail and flicks his wings. Dobs bristles, the red flame gathers in his eyes, he flies at the intruder and a chase begins around the orchard trees near me, three of the other invaders joining in. Apparently they all want to possess the orchard because I am there, for they have not disputed over this territory before. I begin to fear the object for possession that causes much of this strife is myself. When I return to the front garden the Robins follow and sing from trees surrounding me there. This seems to show that territory is not the whole cause of their determination to get near my cottage. A power of reasoning seems indicated, for they all discern where the source of food comes from and wish to secure ME, not only the land for their winter territory.

October 3rd. New Robin now displays a draggled, loose feather, waving behind his rump – a sign of further encounters with Blackcap Robin, who still sings in the adjacent apple-tree. Dobs, looking spick and span, seems now to have settled his disputes. New Robin has gained the west window of the cottage and nearly half the lawn in line with this window. Beyond this he is not allowed to encroach, with one exception. The bird-bath is just inside Dobs's territory. New Robin is allowed an evening bath, taken always *after* Dobs, apparently by arrangement.

The above settlement between New Robin and Dobs proved final. Blackcap Robin was pushed farther away from the cottage by New Robin, and he finally settled at the back of West Garden orchard. The demure-looking south-west Robin held her added portion up to the flower-beds. Dobs was successful in ousting his mate from the kitchen door. She retreated into East Garden and even through the bitter frosts and snows of almost the worst winter within living human memory, she never ventured to seek crumbs from the cottage back door.

The difference in Dobs's method of dealing with each intruder was always noticeable. As my notes reveal, he was constantly on guard against his mate but never attacked her. The means employed to keep her away were calm song, determined and persistent; occasional chasing or very mild display consisting of puffing out his feathers – which to the human eye made him look an important bird not to be disobeyed! Yet he seemed more concerned over keeping the back door from his mate than in attending to west Robin's threats of intrusion on the west side of the cottage. These he settled surprisingly quickly by song sounding fiercer than he ever used for his mate. West Robin and Dobs rolled together under the tree once or twice, but there was not vicious action in this conflict and Dobs's expression did not show fury as with New Robin. With west Robin his song was loud and emphatic, but he never resorted to spluttering notes or hysterical-sounding shrillness. From the first his manner with New Robin was altogether different. Directly he sighted New Robin he became agitated, his eyes flamed, his voice became shrill, he spluttered and used distortion display to its fullest extent. He pounced down and attacked so violently that I had to frighten them apart for fear death would result from his vicious action. But the attention he payed to south-west Robin's encroachment on his land was scarcely worth mentioning, so mild was his expostulation. Going from one to another of all these intruders he always changed tactics according to the individual. This seems to show that display is not only an automatic reaction but a controlled proceeding, used with judgment according to assessment and knowledge of the opponent.

The following autumn, which preceded an exceptionally mild winter, Dobs had an easy time. There were no battles for territory in front of my cottage and his mate retreated to East Garden without giving any trouble. I noticed that Robins were more evenly distributed over uninhabited surrounding land. I comment upon this because the influx of Robins to my garden in autumn has always appeared to be in relation to the hardness of the coming winter. I also notice that Tits and other individuals under close observation will choose more sheltered roosts when bad weather is ahead, although at the time of going to roost no sign is apparent of the sudden change, which comes after midnight. Another case of precognition of weather changes is that they will suddenly eat much more about two days previous to a cold spell. At the time of their sudden appetite the day may be very mild and humans unaware of the severe weather ahead.

CHAPTER 5

Recognition, Friendship and Games

The following spring, although Dobs then had all my front lawn and half the orchard, his mate nested in East Garden. I saw very little of her, but Dobs sought all his food in my garden, only entering East Garden for necessary visits to the nest. On the few occasions when she tried to take food from me Dobs interfered, pouncing down and chasing her away then returning to get some cake himself. If it was the period of feeding his mate he gave the cake to her, but later, when she was feeding the young, he still drove her from me and snatched the food she wanted for her nestlings, either eating it himself or taking it to the young.

It amuses me sometimes to work Dobs up into a fury. I know some of the things that set him off! When many birds are crowding round me, waiting to be handed food, I hold out one bit of cheese to a Tit who quickly takes it from my hand. Then Dobs sees me produce a pellet of bread, which I offer him. His look of anger is worth studying. He stays where he is, glaring at me and watching for cheese to replace the bread. If I then hand a Tit another piece of cheese the fat is in the fire! Dobs starts attacking first one bird then another, charging about like a madman until he has cleared all the birds away. He does not then come and ask for cheese, he is also angry with me, so turns his back with a flick of his tail, shakes his ruffled feathers and flies to a tree where he sings loudly, his back still towards me. After a little he returns in a good mood and even if there are many Tits around he waits very patiently until every bird has had cheese before taking some himself.

He knows I object to his attacking other birds, especially when they are on my hand. These attacks appear to be jealousy, as Robins always like to have the field to themselves. I find all tame ones are liable to sudden tempers when they see other birds on my hand, but this angry charging of other species is quite different from their reaction to another Robin. They try and ward off one of their own species with much display, before it has a chance to perch on my hand.

I find from close observation that birds have no difficulty over recognising and remembering each other individually. They also can distinguish individual humans, as the following will show.

When Dobs's offspring were fledged he tried to prevent their going near me – unlike some parent Robins who have liked me to help feed their young until the time came to drive them away. One of the young from his second brood caused him much trouble and refused to leave for some weeks after Dobs had got rid of the rest of the brood. Whenever chased by his angry parent, Dobs's son flew to the top of my head or avoided trouble by retreating next door until Dobs was out of sight, but little Dobson always returned, especially if I called his name. When his red breast-feathers began to appear Dobs grew really fierce and eventually the youngster had to leave. I completely lost sight of him for nearly three months then news came that a ringed Robin had been seen near a farmhouse about a mile from my cottage. I hurried there and was told the pink-ringed Robin had appeared the previous week when the farmer's wife was mowing the lawn. It had flown along in front of the machine just as the youngster used to do when I was mowing. He had later flown across the lane to a small enclosure and had not been seen since. I went into the enclosure, calling his name. Almost at once Dobson appeared on a tree beside me, his head-feathers raised, his eyes glittering, apparently with excitement. He may also have associated the sight of me with Dobs pouncing on him, hence the raised head-feathers, for I noticed he looked around carefully with an expectant pose and head stretched right up so he could get full view over the branch on which he was perched. Immediately I held out my hand he flew to it with his former confidence, ate some cake and returned to the bough where he warbled a quiet song with eyes fixed upon me. He did not again look around for Dobs – if this was his reason for that action at first – nor were his head-feathers raised any more. When I walked away he hopped to the end of the bough where he could get the best view of my retreating figure; on looking back before turning the corner I saw him craning his neck out to keep me in sight. A month later I went again to visit him. The farmer's wife had once or twice seen him in the interval, but he would not perch on her hand. This time he met me in the lane outside the enclosure as soon as I called his name. He sang a few notes, looking at me with the same excited glint in his eye but this time without raised head-feathers, nor did he stretch up his head to search the distance as before. At once he flew to my hand with accustomed familiarity. Afterwards I visited him at intervals of a month, six weeks and four months, and although my clothes in winter were completely different and new to him, this did not affect his immediate recognition. Once he flew to me in the lane before I called him, proving my voice was not his only means of recognition. He did not always keep to the same part of the enclosure or lane, his winter territory was very extensive and he encroached on that of other Robins at times, especially near the two farmhouses – a second farm being four large fields away from the enclosure he had at first occupied. Several other people, when seeing me with Dobson on my hand in the lane, tried to coax him on to theirs but without success, this leaving no doubt that he remembered and recognised me individually. An interval of eight months had elapsed the last time I passed along Dobson's lane. When near his territory I stopped to talk to someone. A minute later he flew towards me, straightway perching on the hand held out to greet him. He ate ten pieces of cake instead of the usual three or four, his eyes glittered with excitement and his head-feathers were slightly raised as he looked at me and sang subsong perched very near. There were no signs of another Robin in the lane nor did Dobson look around as if expecting one to appear; this time I think the head-feathers were raised because of my presence.

Birds are able to distinguish individual humans from afar, for those that are tamest often fly across meadows and along roads to meet me, apparently spotting me from tree-tops. It is not my clothes that are responsible for their ability to recognise me, for on one occasion I left home by the road, wearing a blue coat and head-scarf and returned across fieldpaths in a green mackintosh and hood, purposely pulled low over my face. Both had been purchased while out, but the birds flew as usual to meet me, recognising me from across two long fields. In winter, when very hungry, several Great Tits have sometimes flown to a nearby bus stop to meet my return bus on the rare occasions when I take this double-decker which passes my house to the county town. I presume they watch me get into it and remember this when two hours later the bus returns.

Close watch is kept over all my movements, and I find they often know what I am going to do from seeing my preparations. For instance, one winter when my hot-water supply failed I took weekly afternoon baths at a friend's house. After the third time Great and Blue Tits had learnt where I was going when they saw my basket filled with bath gear; directly I started out they flew on in front, along and across the road, and perched in my friend's garden to await my arrival, their purpose being to get a feed from my hand before I disappeared. (Wherever I go the Tit-box is taken, so they are not disappointed when they do clever things.) The birds never flew in advance to this house except when I went out prepared for a bath.

Their reaction to humans varies according to the person. Some people who come to my cottage always induce fear, others they treat with comparative friendliness and enter the room while they are there without concern, although they never behave quite normally until alone with me again. Two people entering the room generally frightens them away for a few minutes, and it takes them longer to gain courage to enter again when two people are with me than when there is only one. Three strangers they fear still more, which shows that up to a point they are aware of numbers. This applies to whether the people are speaking and moving or quiet and still, it seeming the sight of the extra person that disturbs them. There have been some exceptional occasions when birds have entered the room confidently before two or even four strangers, and it is curious to find that their reactions to people are frequently in sympathy with my thoughts.

Among themselves they also have likes and dislikes. Sometimes special friendships between the young of a brood are formed as soon as they leave the nest, if not before. The two birds become inseparable companions, doing everything together until one or both leave the territory. Twist and her sister was one example of this – page 26. Two fledgling male Great Tits were another example. They were like twins, indistinguishable from each other in appearance and always together. Among their games was the following, played with much twittering. One twin would lightly touch the tip of his brother's wing, which sent him hopping quickly a few twigs away – this game being always played in the trees. Twin I followed him, twittering excitedly and again touched his wing-tip, the game continuing like this until Twin II, with much sign of merriment, changed over and became the toucher. Fledgling Great Tits, when playing with each other, have a delightful laughter note, soft but unmistakably the excited chuckling of enjoyment over their game. This note is not used for other occasions. The Twins were always playing together with 'laughter-notes' and I never saw them apart until one day an accident happened to one of the brothers. All day long he had to keep quiet and still, holding a broken leg tucked between feathers underneath him. This puzzled his brother, who at first kept trying to entice him to play by touching his wing-tips and pulling his tail. Then he attempted to pull the injured leg down in a gently playful manner. This obviously hurt the injury and brought a sharp scold-note and peck of reproval. The uninjured Twin stared a moment in apparent astonishment then flew away, all playfulness gone from his ways. After this he kept apart from his brother and moped by himself with as forlorn an air as the twin who had suffered the fracture. I once saw him place food within reach of his injured brother, afterwards quickly flying away. In ten days the fracture was healed but a callus, looking like a false joint, had formed in the centre of the tarsus, the lower half being set out of line. The leg seemed strong and normal except in appearance. The brothers never resumed their friendship, both seemed dissatisfied with remaining in my garden and they left separately, first the one who had been injured, a week later his brother.

In winter, two years later, a strange-looking Great Tit appeared, with feathers artificially blackened as if he had been bathing in black ink. He flew straight to my hand, as if he had never been away, the peculiarity of his crooked leg making identification unmistakable. He disappeared again in spring and never returned. This was a good test of bird memory. I think those who are tame when very young never forget. This may account for some old, ill or injured birds who occasionally appear on my doorstep, astonishing me by coming straight to my hand. I have lost identification of the individual but their memory serves them well when needing help.

I find the various males and females of my garden know each other even at a distance, also, the males who are mated never respond to the mating signals of a female not their own although they may watch her with interest. In a garden like mine, where as many as possible of each species stay to nest after winter hospitality, their territory is generally not large, so frequently males come into contact with females mated to a neighbouring male. The Chaffinch is the only species in my garden who has attempted coition with a female who was not his mate. She was slightly injured and had difficulty in flying. The Chaffinch pursued her on the ground, uttering the note peculiar to mating season. She tried to dodge him, but he got on her back and was shaken off. He became persistent and I interfered, the male then returned to his own mate.

Parent birds also never mistake fledglings of a neighbouring brood for their own. They will sometimes show concern for a straying youngster of a very tender age, but older fledglings are generally chased away if they are of an age when their parents still feed them.

Birds, like humans, need occupation as an outlet for their vitality and for a pastime. Many Great Tits are indoors with me for much of the time during autumn and winter, and I find it necessary to provide toys for them, otherwise they choose a pastime that inflicts damage to something of value to me. Before I knew that Great Tits liked toys I found one of four celluloid parakeets (from a Christmas tree) missing from its perch on a holly bough in my room. That same day I saw a Great Tit fly to the holly, knock one of the remaining parakeets on to the floor, then, holding it with one foot, begin hammering, pecking and pulling the bird in mock-ferocious manner, often picking it up and turning it over, probably because this made it rattle. Having succeeded in tearing its side open, the Tit flew with it out of the window. Until all these toy birds had been disposed of, the Tit had no eye for anything else in the room. Some clever imitations of Blue Tits, made in felt, were ill-treated in the same manner, but if nothing as realistic and exciting is in sight, Great Tits will seize my ink-bottle stopper and, knowing this to be forbidden, fly quickly out of the window with it while I am filling my pen. When wanting to cork the bottle I see the Tit on the lawn or a tree branch, ill-treating the stopper like he did the toy parakeets and stuffed birds. These were not regarded as live things, merely as toys that amused him and something on which to vent high spirits. Their violent attacks upon these toy birds had resemblance to the reactions some birds show to stuffed hawks.

Unfortunately, it is not only the ink-bottle stopper they destroy. When they see me writing, dipping my pen in the ink-pot, their favourite way of attracting my attention is to upset the ink. They do it deliberately, then escape my wrath by quick flight out of the window. They have various ways of trying to divert me from writing, often hammering on my skull, and sitting on my shoulder to pull my hair and tweak my ears, this meaning they want nuts and cheese. If I refuse to be bullied into noticing them sometimes one of them will walk on to my page and carefully lift my nib from the paper, looking up at me while doing it. This forces me to stop, so the Tits have won! The writing of this book provides good Tit sport. Many of my notes are on loose sheets; these they watch me place in order on the table beside the typewriter, then they fly up and purposely scatter pages to the floor. They have developed a technique for upsetting things by landing with a rush and quick skidding of their feet. Together with the breeze made by their wings, it scatters pages with effective speed; also, large cake-tins they send crashing to the floor by this quick skidding method; with luck the lid falls off through the force of the crash and after a hasty flight to the window, because of the noise – they return to eat the contents of the tin. Another game is to perch on the roller of the typewriter when I pause for thought, and if my hands are not held over the page, they tear a hole in the last sentence while I am thinking of the next! Occasionally a Tit taps a key sharply with his beak but, luckily, the resulting movement he finds alarming.

Close observation of bird-life reveals that many species, especially when young, spend much time in play. The young of some species associate with other species in chasing games and other recreation. Especially young Willow-Warblers and sometimes Chiffchaffs, delight in chasing other species, often much to their annoyance. A Blue Tit is the Willow-Warbler's favourite for this game, perhaps because this Tit is responsive. In my orchard I have seen these two chasing each other around the trees until the Blue Tit, less active on the wing, retired to rest. The young Willow-Warbler paused only a moment to look for the next most suitable victim. He saw a Spotted Flycatcher perched on the fence with dark eyes intent on choosing a fly, a bird light on the wing and worthy of chase. Before the chosen fly could be snapped the Willow-Warbler was after him, the sober grey Flycatcher swift and silent in flight, the sprightly young Willow Warbler, in fresh plumage of primrose and green, noisily snapping his beak as with agile flight he chased the Flycatcher around trees and across the orchard. Directly the Flycatcher alighted on another perch, the Willow-Warbler turned to race after a Chaffinch who was pursuing his mate. But the Chaffinch was engrossed in his own affairs so attention was turned to a Great Tit, flying from her nest to find food for her young. The Tit scolded angrily for parent birds have no time for play. The game often lasts a considerable time with scarcely a break, for when other birds fail there is always a Sparrow to chase.

Occasionally Willow-Warblers and Chiffchaffs will keep to their species for the chasing game, but usually in their case, a different species is chosen for play. When chasing Swallows the Willow-Warbler meets his match in sharp turns of the wing and swiftness of flight. One day five baby Swallows were perched close together on the wire outside my window. A young Willow-Warbler was perched on the tree nearby, watching as eagerly as the baby Swallows for the parent birds to fly back with food. Each time they returned, the teasing Willow-Warbler chased them, making so much confusion that the Swallows dropped half their beakful of flies in their haste to stuff them down the babies' throats and get away from the Willow-Warbler. Sometimes the Swallows snapped at the teasing imp but it made no difference. The Willow-Warbler seemed in his element, matching his swift flight against a Swallow's. The plumage of these two species made a lovely contrast; the delicate spring-like colouring of the small, slight Warbler against the deep night-blue of the larger long-winged bird. Yet the Willow-Warbler's wings sped him as quickly as the Swallow's longer ones. This can only be for short flights, the Warbler putting forth all his strength.

Swallows and Swifts, in chasing games, keep to their own species. I have seen Swallows play a wonderfully graceful game of catching a feather. It was one August afternoon when I was sitting at the top of a steeply sloping farm field in the uplands of Devon that I noticed more Swallows than usual were wheeling close together over one part of the field, presumably an abundance of flies on the hot, sunny day being the cause. Ducks and Geese roamed in this field and the grass was sprinkled with a few white breast-feathers. I then saw a Swallow dip to the ground and sweep upwards with one of these feathers held in his beak and, circling above the other Swallows, he let it fall. As it floated down it was caught by one of the wheeling birds who then rose above the rest and again the feather was let loose, to float down through the many circling Swallows. This time it nearly reached earth, then one bird swept down with graceful dip and flicker of wings, rising aloft with the feather, to drop it once more. Sometimes their wayward toy would fall uncaught, perhaps too worn for further use; then quickly a bird swooped to the grass, seized another feather while on the wing and the play continued as before. It was a beautiful game to watch in the setting of hills, with a background of wild moorland and far away the blue haze of distant sea meeting the deeper blue sky.

The Swallow's game may be evolved from the simple one, common to many species, of picking up things, dropping and watching them fall, although I have never seen a Swallow do this. An untamed Jackdaw once took a fancy for entering my bedroom down the chimney at dawn. Several mornings he came, and getting familiar with the room, he flew to my dressing-table. In spite of difficulty in balancing on the polished surface, he skidded about and picked up small things, dropped them over the table edge and turned his head sideways with an intent expression, to watch them fall. Eventually, he knocked over a photograph frame, and the crash sent him flying out of the window.

One of my Great Tits' toys is a covered glass jar containing seashells. They pluck off the lid, pick out the shells and chuck them with a sharp twist of their heads either down on the floor or across the room, always watching them fall with interest. Matches are treated in the same manner and often when I have been out I return to find matches strewn all over the room, the box having been pulled open and lying in two halves on the floor.

One of the great charms of House-Martins is their playfulness. They have fun even in the cradle. I have watched a young one stretching half its body out of the nest to play with a smaller Martin in a neighbouring nest. Twittering excitedly, with head craned forward, it just managed to touch the tip of the other baby's beak. The smaller one entered into the fun and bobbed up from its nest to take the kiss, both withdrawing directly afterwards. Then the bigger one, behaving excitedly, began poking its brother – or sister – as if trying to egg it on to join in the fun, but getting no response, the merry Martin again turned to the neighbouring baby and, with a terrific effort, heaved almost all its body outside the nest, with eager twitterings touching the small one's beak. This touch or kiss was received with obvious amusement by the little one, who repeatedly retired into its nest then bobbed up again to thrust its head forward for another touch of beaks. The game continued for some time, the enjoyment of the Martins so infectious it was impossible to watch without laughter. The elder one, in its eager excitement, made stretching efforts that could easily end in falling from the nest and the parents evidently disapproved. When preparing for their second brood they wisely sealed up the old entrance hole, making another on the opposite side of their nest where there were no neighbours, so the young of their next brood were not tempted to play risky games with neighbouring young before they were fledged.

Many birds play in a puppy-like manner at shaking and biting of things inedible. I once watched a young Herring-Gull on the bank of a Cornish estuary treating my small umbrella in this manner. After a droll examination he played for a long while at shaking and biting it, then began pulling and letting go the elastic band, watching the effect with keen interest. Previously he had investigated my satchel, pulled out the contents, discarded some sketching materials but seized upon my lunch, taking a bite from a sandwich which he surprisingly spat out – this was before food rationing! His attention then turned to my bare legs which he pecked several times and the buttons on my plim-soles catching his eye, he tried to pull them off, diving first at one shoe then the other in playful manner. When tired of playing with the umbrella he fell asleep beside it, enabling me to make a quick sketch of him before he awoke. I learnt afterwards the explanation of his tame-ness. A month or two previously he had been rescued from the river, coated in oil and unable to fly. Someone had cared for him, cleaned his feathers and given him food.

Although the Song-Thrush is not a playful bird, a youngster in my garden spent so much time shaking and pulling at some rope attached to a stick that he unravelled it, and I removed the rope lest he entan-gled himself.

The Blackbird is an individualist in all his ways. His idea of a game seems to be property ownership, and he plays with a chosen friend. If either friend is prevented from playing, the game does not continue with another Blackbird neighbour. For three years, at all seasons, one Blackbird in my orchard played with a neighbour friend at owning a small tree-stump. As the stump was the opposite side of the orchard to the neighbour's territory, this was not a dispute for land but a game that both birds appeared to enjoy spending much time over every day. Even in nesting season they played for a short while in the evenings. If the neighbour did not turn up, my Blackbird flew next door and they returned together to the tree-stump. The game began by typical Blackbird stalking, taking turns to be leader or follower. Then one

bird flew onto the tree-stump, the other quickly chased him off and
perched there himself, with tail outspread, head upturned and humorous cockiness in his erect posture. In his turn he was chased off, the
stalking began again and the game was repeated, often continuing for
hours with slight variations. There was some resemblance to the children's game of 'I'm the King of the Castle.' I have seen many other
male Blackbirds at similar play, always with a chosen friend, other
neighbours just as accessible being treated differently and generally
chased right off the territory. Darky and Oakleaf were another
example of this (page 59).

In all these things there is much evidence that the mind of a bird
works according to the individual as well as to the species.

Birds sunbathe frequently in summer and autumn, often using certain sheltered tree-stumps or dead branches for this purpose. In my
orchard a half-fallen, dead apple-tree is one of the chosen sun-traps. I
first discovered this one midsummerday morning, just as the sun
reached its zenith. In the leafy orchard, where the grass was almost
shoulder high, this half-fallen, bare-branched tree stood out like a grey
rock does in a deep green sea. Along its sloping trunk and bare arms
there were several sunbathing birds lying flat on their breasts, their
wings and tails outspread so each feather shone with the full light of
sunshine. Their heads were all turned to one side and slightly raised to
the sun, their beaks held half-open as if to let the sun shine inside too.
Three Willow-Warblers were on the upper branch, some Great Tits
and Blue Tits lay on the gnarled stump, while the thick base of the
sloping trunk had been chosen by two young Blackbirds.

Sometimes a familiar bird will spread wings and tail to sunbathe on
my lap or in the crook of my arm. Every feather on the head and body
is raised and the beak is always held half-open, perhaps for breathing
reasons, as in heat waves they occasionally fly about with beaks agape.
Goldfinches in sunbathing pose are a very lovely sight.

I once saw two Herons sunbathing in a buttercup meadow, near a
river. Their long necks were stretched out to the full and pointed
upwards with heads held aslant and beaks open, their half-spread
wings held low and away from their sides. Against the golden background in the bright sunlight these queer, white, snake-like necks,
toning into pale grey at the back, looked indescribably odd. They
remained motionless for so long that it seemed they were not birds

but some form of symbolic statue, expressing something weird and remote.

Along that same river there were Lapwing and Redshank associating in mixed parties, bathing and splashing together in the shallows and sunning themselves side by side on the stones at the water's edge. Certain striking contrasts in these two species make this friendly association very beautiful to watch. I made the following notes at the time – Lapwing hover with flapping wings and legs dangling over the silken sheen of the water which reflects them perfectly. How they enjoy the water, bathing and splashing then shaking their ragged wings to dry. Some chasing each other excitedly and tumbling close above the water with wild, wailing cries, sweeping upwards in a curve then dropping sheer, wings aslant, broad petalled and ragged tipped as if torn by winds. The Redshanks are slick in flight, their clean-cut, pointed wings taking them with swift precision. They call in pure, liquid sounding notes while skimming the water's surface in rapid zigzag shoots, or swinging upwards in wide sweeping curves, over and down the grassy bank, their legs sticking out behind like little tongues of flame. They perch among shining wet stones at the water's edge, suddenly becoming almost invisible, their colouring changed from the dazzling white and tortoiseshell shades seen in flight, to a dull greyish tone, matching the stone's shadows. They pause motionless for a while as if dozing, then suddenly one or two arise, shoot across the river, calling and trilling; others follow in twos or threes to settle elsewhere and, when they alight, their long wings are held suspended upwards a moment then folded in orderly manner by bringing them forward, round and down to their sides.

Flight and song is used by many species as their principal form of recreation. This will be referred to in separate chapters.

CHAPTER 6

Roosts, Food, and Nesting-Boxes

Birds look ahead more than is generally supposed. They often hunt for and test roosts in the morning; if the roost is later occupied by another bird, fighting will follow with fierce attack by the original owner and poor defence by the new occupant. Once a Great Tit, hard up for a bed, found a Blue Tit roosting in a box hung to the window-frame. He went through threatening fight displays and pecked the Blue Tit in her bed. She put up hot defence, the Great Tit failed to get the roost so flew away. Soon he came back and started a violent attack on the box from the back end, where the wood had rotted and was reinforced with cardboard. His onslaught was effective, the back end gave way and the Blue Tit was forced to leave her roost; so did the Great Tit, for it was now of doubtful value. I hastily repaired the damage. The Great Tit immediately flew up and sat inside the box. Blue Tit followed, squealing loudly and butting with lowered head at the Great Tit in the usual manner of 'Billy Biter' when determined to win a fight. The Great Tit did not defend himself, and in a few seconds flew off, the Blue Tit entering her roost. It seemed the Great Tit knew he had done wrong; all his fury was spent, he looked guilty and drooped his tail as he flew away. On following evenings he made a habit of peering inside the roost to make sure the Blue Tit was there; she always was, so he hopped on to the roof, gave one or two sharp raps, as if for fun, then flew elsewhere to bed. Sometimes he glanced with a queer expression at the back end before leaving the box, perhaps remembering but never repeating his onslaught.

Where to find safe shelter for the night is the first great problem the young fledgling has to face. One morning I watched a young Great Tit spend a long time trying to widen a narrow hole in a tree. He managed to get out a few bits of rotten wood, but his beak was not yet strong enough for the job and he could not widen the hole sufficiently for turning round inside it; a bird will not roost back to the opening. There was only one possible solution for the young Tit, he tried entering the hole backwards. It was amusing to watch his efforts, for steering the tip of his long tail into the opening proved very difficult and he went through many antics, always with his head turned round to keep an eye on the troublesome tail, before he successfully got the tip into the hole. Then he slowly squeezed the rest of his body backwards along the narrow, level crevice. It was obviously a tight fit and his head came too near the entrance for safety as a roost, but he stayed there for some minutes then came out and went in search of a better one, which later was found and he slept in it at night. He had worked very hard for his bed.

I sometimes find the smallest member of a newly-fledged brood – various species – at dusk seeking cover on the ground under leaves of plants or old tree-roots. Its parents make every effort to entice it to safe roosting perches, but the fledgling perhaps feels the earth provides more warmth and shelter from wind. I have tried placing these small fledglings on safe tree-perches, thinking their difficulty might be to fly upwards, but they leave the high perch and immediately seek ground cover again, although they are birds of the trees. They seem not to have instinctive feeling for roosting above ground, but gradually learn to find safe cover at night in such places as are typical of the species.

One evening at dusk, ten-thirty Double Summer Time, I had just got into bed when a baby Great Tit, with a tail barely a quarter of an inch long, fluttered in through the window and settled on my chest. After close inspection of my face it cuddled down within an inch of my chin, head tucked under wing. It was such a tiny ball of fluffed-out feathers and light as thistle-down. After a while I tried to lift without wakening it, but resenting interference, it quickly scrambled still farther underneath my chin, so my head had to be held up while it continued to sleep for an hour. Then I made another attempt to lift it, but at the first touch it fluttered to my shoulder, falling asleep again instantaneously. Finally, I put it into a little box by my bed. This was not to its liking, it became wide awake, flew to the window and slept until dawn, clinging to the inside of the frame, then I put it outside so it could join the rest of the brood. (It was one of Jane's smallest from a second brood.)

Blue Tits have less difficulty in finding a roost because, being so small, they can squeeze into such narrow crevices. But the very young fledgling sometimes underestimates its size. One evening at sun-down nine babies fluttered into my sitting-room and tried to find roosts in cracks of doors or other such crevices too narrow even for a newly-fledged Blue Tit. One fluttered up to my handbag which hung on a door handle, and made many comical efforts to squeeze itself under the flap. This also was unsuccessful so the whole brood trooped out again with much chatter, and were led by their parents to the trees.

Sometimes it happens that one of my youngster Great Tits, instead of coming to his accustomed roost in a box on the picture rails above my bed, goes off roaming in the early hours of evening and does not get back till morning. Directly he enters the room – about 7.30 a.m. – he flies straight to his bed and stays there some minutes, perhaps having missed the comfortable roost on his night out! He goes early to bed that evening.

There is much variation in the hours birds go to roost. Some individuals in a species seem to need more sleep than others, they not only go to bed sooner, but often sleep later in the morning. With Great Tits the variation may be as much as two hours – this having nothing to do with age. Some also sleep more soundly and wake up less often in the night. Curley, for instance, slept through the short summer night without once moving on her perch, while others may turn about many times, even pecking the bottom of their roosts in the night. Curley was the first to sleep above my bed on the picture rail; soon both my sitting-room and bedroom had young Great Tits roosting along the rails, the corners being favoured and fought for. One night Curley fell from her perch in her sleep, for the rail is slippery and no interlock of feet is possible. She was rather frightened for a moment, but directly I turned on the light she flew up to the rail again and slept. Next night I gave her a cardboard box on the picture rail, many more of these afterwards supplied to meet the Tits' demands. Instead of hanging pictures on my rails, the walls are hung with sugar and cereal cartons; often by day the Tits hammer on these boxes in play and make holes in the roofs of their roosts, but I never interfere as it keeps them employed upon damaging their own beds instead of my curtains, arm-chairs and other furniture, which they pull to bits. They become very possessive over these boxes and the owners fly at any other Tit who by day hammers at the cardboard for fun. After they have grown adult plumage they dislike sleeping near each other and short squabbles arise every evening over the roosting-boxes. Those most determined to remain take possession of the rooms, and the others are driven away by degrees. If the weather is very bad some often return to their old boxes and no squabbling occurs, those who have taken possession becoming tolerant. Great Tits are so individual that there is an infinite amount of variety over roosting behaviour as in everything else they do, this making it very interesting to watch. At daybreak every morning I waken to the sound of birds' wings as they flutter through the darkened room and fly out of the window over the top of drawn curtains.

One wet winter night at one o'clock, a very strong wind arose, driving the rain through the open window. I got up, turned on the light and my hand was on the latch to close the fanlight window when one of my Great Tits flew in from the dark night and went straight to his roosting-box above my bed. It was a strange and lovely sensation to see a bird fly in from the darkness of the wild, wet night.

In autumn and winter my male Blackbird, Darky, and his mate sometimes take no notice of each other during the daytime, but this is what I often see at roost hour. The female appears on the lawn at sundown, looks up at a tree, gives a few wing twitches or cocks her tail upwards. Darky then flies down to a different part of the lawn, he eyes her from the distance. Both feed for a while then she flies to roost in a macrocarpus near my window. He slightly tilts his head towards her, showing consciousness of her movement, but continues to feed and hop around the lawn in the fading light. Eventually he flies to roost on another branch of the same tree. She may go to bed half an hour before him or wait until dusk, he following almost immediately afterwards, for roosting hours vary. Weather affects this, also if there are other Blackbirds on the lawn they stay longer, perhaps finding their presence of interest. I made the following notes on September 23rd. – At sundown, seven Blackbirds were feeding on the lawn until too dark to distinguish young birds from old, or sexes. They flitted about with quick movements, in the darkness looking like a lot of gnomes, fascinating to watch. Suddenly one bird struck up a piercing 'tchink, tchink' and still 'tchinking,' he flew to roost in the macrocarpus. Directly he flew up all the rest flitted silently away to bed. It is the first time this autumn that roosting has been advertised by this call; probably it now will continue, roosting territory being of importance in autumn and winter.

On the rare occasions when I get on my bed in the afternoon, the Great Tit who sleeps above me perches for a moment on the screen beside the bed, surveying my recumbent form; then he flies to his roost on the picture rail above. I hear him give a few preening movements before he settles down quietly for about three minutes. After that he becomes restless, begins tapping the bottom of his bed in play, then flies off out of the window or comes down to my bed to amuse himself. The birds appear to regard the bed as my nest, for I have sometimes had twenty or more playing on it when I have been ill and, instead of making messes on sheets and blankets, they fly to the window-sill or screen, where newspaper is spread for sanitary purposes, returning again to the bed directly afterwards. Only if they are suddenly annoyed or I speak to them severely for tearing at my book or pulling a blanket to pieces, they retort by making an immediate mess on the bed then flying to the window. They never play about on the bed unless I am on it.

One winter, when I was ill for two or three weeks, Tits amused themselves on the bed every day in a variety of ways. Some played at possession of me, so it seemed, and displayed while walking about all over me, tails fully spread, wings half-opened and drooped, heads stiffly held up, their beaks pointing to the ceiling. They muttered queer language to each other while displaying, and their expressions were so humorous it was impossible to watch without laughter. It was obviously all in fun, the birds entering into the game were not at that time disputing for territory, for it was early winter. Another amusement was to slide down the slopes of my pillow, which miniature alpine sport some seemed to enjoy. They climbed to the top, then slowly slid down without moving their feet. Occasionally they rolled on the bed, two together with feet interlocked, quarrelling over a piece of cheese. They became very tyrannical when I had no more cheese to give them, especially Baldhead, who is a determined bird with a sharp beak. When he stood over me with his threatening look, demanding what I was unable to give, there was need for complete submergence under bedclothes. If I put out my head to breathe he pounced at my nose and gave a few sharp pecks to my cheeks so the sheet had to be quickly pulled over my head again. But his wits were as sharp as his beak; he tried to get at me by tugging at the top of the sheet, lifting the edge and squeezing himself underneath until he reached my hair which he pulled vigorously, while the other Tits walked over the sheet above my face, giving occasional pecks to try to remove it. This type of treatment is always inflicted upon me when my supply of cheese and nuts runs out — in these days of rationing and food scarcity too often occurring.

If they think I have any peanuts they start chucking away other food given them and pester me persistantly for nuts until I take them to the cupboard where these are usually kept, and let them see for themselves the nut-tin is empty. They then understand and remember there are none until they see a fresh supply arrive. When Baldhead is shown the empty tin he looks very cross, the sudden change in his expression very noticeable, and he flies out of the window with a peculiar twitch of his tail which he gives when annoyed. But he soon returns to perch on my shoulder and accept some cheese. I used to keep the few peanuts obtainable in a table-drawer, but some of the Great Tits found a way of getting at them, even when it was closed. They climbed up underneath the table and entered the back end of the drawer, pulled out some of the many folded papers and letters which blocked their way and heaved these over the back-end to the floor. This was a hard struggle and took them many minutes. Then they squeezed themselves along the drawer from the back to the front, where the nuts were kept. It was an astonishing feat, for the folded papers almost filled the rather long but narrow drawer. They deserved the nuts for their effort, but because the floor was always being littered with papers, that had to be replaced in the drawer many times a day, I had to keep their nuts elsewhere.

When my Great Tits want to get a nut that I am gripping firmly between my fingers, they first make efforts to pull it out, if this fails to release my hold they try to pull my fingers away from the nut, between whiles throwing me many impatient glances.

Birds, like humans, have individual tastes in food. One Thrush likes dried currants but will not eat bread unless snow covers the ground and he is desperately hungry; another Thrush refuses currants and likes bread. One Blackbird would not eat worms but lived on insects, fruit, etc. Darky sometimes eats a wasp after pulling out the sting, but I have never seen one eaten by any other Blackbird. Great Tits eat bees;

only one of my many Great Tits likes wasps; the sting of bees and wasps they always extract with much dexterity before eating.

Once I watched a youngster Great Tit cautiously approach a huge Bumble-Bee, gorging a fallen pear on the lawn. After a moment's hesitation the Tit gently tapped the bee's furry body with his beak. It made an angry buzz and tried to fly but could only crawl, which it did apace, the Tit hopping close behind and repeatedly prodding it on the back. They went half-way across the lawn in this manner, then the bee flew heavily away; the Tit gazed after it and gave a double-noted call. The young Great Tit is full of fun and curiosity; this incident, which was amusing to watch, had no connection with food, he was playing with the bee and, judging by his expression and manner, he was sorry when he lost his toy. They never eat Bumble-Bees.

Cheese is a popular food with Tits as with most birds, yet one or two Great Tits refuse it, liking animal fat and nuts, while another likes cheese but will not eat animal fat. Weather affects their choice of food. In cold spells they want more fat and cheese, in hot weather fat is not eaten, but heat does not put them off cheese and nuts. A few are fussy over the type of nut, but I have never yet had a Tit refuse peanuts. I recently obtained a coconut, for the first time since the war; the Tits looked at it nervously and did not begin to peck it until two hours after I hung it outside. Even when they did try eating it, to my surprise many of them were not keen on this type of nut; two or three Great Tits made a grimace and wiped their bills after pecking it, not returning for more. My birds are all well fed, probably they would devour the coconut if very hungry. I found the Blue Tits liked it better than the Great Tits, but even the Blue Tits were very moderate in the amount they ate, and they took plenty of bread and fat in proportion to the coconut. I believe the latter is rather indigestible food for birds and when giving one to the Tits care should be taken to supply fat and bread as well, otherwise from hunger they may eat too much of a food that is not good for them in large quantities.

I have some Great Tits who are fussy over the type of cheese I offer them. Process or Dutch is taken up and chucked across the room, while the kind to their taste is eaten with relish. A few individuals seem unable to digest fat. It is harmful to give this to small nestlings, especially Great Tits and probably all species of Tit nestlings. I once had a pair of Great Tits who fed their brood with much enthusiasm on large quantities of mutton fat. To my horror as well as the parents' distress, the nestlings never grew any feathers of the normal kind. When it was time for them to leave the nest they clambered out and fell to the ground, unable to fly. They were horrible-looking objects, duncoloured and looking as if they had been dipped in grease, their undeveloped quills without a single coloured feather. Only three left the nest, I presume the others had died beforehand. These miserable fledglings were devoured by cats within half an hour. Their inexperienced but enthusiastic parents were both first-year birds – I also was ignorant over nestling diet in those days. This is the only case among all my birds, even first-year couples, of mistaken choice over food for their young. Always they give natural food entirely for the first few days after hatching, then they may add a little cheese, gradually increasing this. Tits will not give the nestlings any other artificial food except cheese or carefully selected peanuts, which they first chew into small fragments. In bad weather Great Tits sometimes overdo the amount of cheese they give their nestlings, with the result the babies shut their beaks tight, refusing to be cajoled into swallowing any more. The parent gives a gentle scold-note, tries every member of the brood, and if with no response, scolds them softly again and leaves the nest, either eating the cheese or chucking it away. Then the parent goes in search of a caterpillar, which the nestlings usually accept, but if too gorged with cheese even to manage this natural food, the parent leaves them for a while until their appetite returns. They are more careful afterwards not to overdo cheese, learning from experience. The same sort of thing happens with Blackbirds, but it is always the father bird who overdoes artificial food. I sometimes watch him trying, for five minutes on end, to stuff bread down a fledgling's closed beak, when it has been so overgorged with this type of food that it tries to escape its tiresome parent by flying away, but the father pursues it and persistently proffers the unwanted bread. Eventually the parent picks up an insect and this is generally accepted. The father Blackbird does not behave with quick understanding like the Great Tit parents, but he learns slowly what the Tit grasps at once.

There was an experiment made of trying to rear Bearded Tits in captivity. Here the parents behaved abnormally, as in most cases of birds who are not free. When their nestlings, from being overfed, did not open their beaks to take food, the parents cast them from the nest instead of waiting for them to get hungry again as my parent Tits have always done. The Tit nestling, if healthy, digests its food so quickly that it very soon gets an appetite again even if overfed; the Bearded Tits' nestlings may perhaps have been unhealthy through unsuitable food in captivity.

Robins and Sparrows seem to thrive on artificial food after the first few days. When Dobs's young are a week old he grabs all he can get of cake, bread, cheese, fat or lean meat, currants and sultanas, etc., and stuffs it down the throats of his nestlings; they never seem to refuse anything. The young Thrush seems not to thrive on such a diet and soon begins to spit out artificial food, gaping again at its parent who quickly seems to understand. Often in droughts, when there are few snails or worms obtainable, my young Thrushes will squat on the ground so their parents can more quickly pop quantities of ants into their beaks.

When I started putting up nesting-boxes for the birds I did not clean the used ones, thinking they would prefer them left undisturbed. Experience taught me this was wrong. I found the Tits who used uncleaned boxes were very restless at night and continually woke up to preen, while those from clean boxes were free of parasite troubles and never needed night preening. I used to watch Tits go to their uncleaned nesting-boxes, peep inside then hurriedly make one or two preening movements and fly away without entering. On examining the boxes I saw lice round the interior of the entrance hole. Directly I cleaned the boxes (a kettle of quite boiling water poured over all sides the surest and quickest method), the Tits occupied the boxes, and preening movements were not again made on looking inside. All the boxes I clean are used for roosting in winter and nesting in spring, those left uncleaned are not entered again, unless driven by necessity through scarcity of safe nesting-holes. Some people think 'leaving it to Nature' is best. But in supplying birds with artificial water-tight boxes we encourage them to use something not quite natural. The hole in a tree probably gets enough moisture through it for cleansing purposes. Also, I notice ants enter tree-holes where Tits have nested, not to nest there themselves, but for some definite reason. This, I think, may be for eating the lice. I have good reason for thinking this as the other day, when cleaning out the Tits' roost-boxes, some ants appeared and I watched them walk off with the bird lice I was scraping out of one of the boxes. Many species of birds, when suffering from this pest, pick up ants and place them between their feathers.

It is important to have the entrance hole of a nesting-box not less than nine inches from the bottom, for the cat's paw, when determined to claw out nestlings, is long and supple. The Blue Tit incident related on page 5 of Chapter 1 could only be accounted for by a cat getting at the nest; here the hole was five inches from the bottom. I have seen a cat get its paw to the nest of a six-inch length also. Since I took to making them at least nine inches there has been no more trouble with marauders. Tits like to have two or three inches of moss foundation to their nest so that, even apart from cats, the deeper boxes are much better. The young are apt to clamber out too soon if they have an entrance hole within easy reach from their nest, and an extra day or two in the box means their chance of surviving is more than doubled, for the fledgling weak on the wing is sure prey for its many enemies. They like plenty of room to stretch their wings before they fly, so the box should not be cramped in width. I make mine about seven inches by five inches or larger. Petrol cans are popular with Tits and I have had several occupied, but the young are, I think, better off in wooden boxes. Unless shaded from the sun, nest boxes should not face south or west. I find sunlight on the entrance hole late in the day encourages the young to flight at the wrong hour. Parents like them to fly from the nest early in the day, this giving time for them to find their feet and learn a little about safe perches before roost hour.

People frequently bring me birds they have picked up; some are badly injured, but more often they are suffering from a minor injury with shock and they would have recovered soon if left on a safe perch close to where found. The fright of unaccustomed human handling and being taken away from its home, although kindly meant, often results in its death. Sometimes, too, the bird brought me is merely an immature fledgling, which always is better left in a hedge or bush close to where it is found. If taken away from its parents it has little chance of survival for it is deprived of its natural food. People sometimes have told me they tried to revive the injured bird by giving it brandy, but this is very bad for birds. Water should be given as soon as possible and a little later some milk, bread, dipped in milk, and cheese, grated or broken into very small fragments. The bird may not be able to eat for a time, but the food can be left within its reach and then the quieter it is, the more chance it will have of recovery. The wild bird does not understand caresses, so there should be no petting and stroking of feathers. This may only aggravate the bird's fright. Alcohol is considered very bad for human beings in cases of head injuries, and it should be remembered that the same applies to birds, whatever their injury, but especially this should not be given to them when stunned.

CHAPTER 7

Finches and Others

BULLFINCH

Bullfinches inhabit my garden for the larger part of the year, only wandering farther afield during autumn and early winter when I do not see them for a few weeks. One spring I made the following notes of my Bullfinch, called Chanter because he sang a lovely little chant.

March 22nd. This morning I heard Chanter calling unusually loudly from the trees, so went out to watch. He flew round the garden, perching conspicuously on the tallest tree-tops, calling his loudest while jerking his tail and lifting his head, showing the full beauty of his glowing breast which was lit to intense brilliance by sunshine. Presently another Bullfinch appeared, I think Chanter's son for this male has always accompanied him and his mate since last summer. He flew close to Chanter, perching opposite him on the branch and seeming to communicate something to him. Chanter nodded his head several times while jerking his tail rapidly. Both birds then nodded, facing each other with heads nearly touching. Then the second Bullfinch flew off, over the trees to a meadow beyond. My instant impression was that this little ceremony meant they were parting company – whether correct or not the other Bullfinch was not again seen in my garden. Chanter's loud call-notes were resumed and soon his mate appeared on an adjoining tree. He flew towards her and perched on a bough a few feet away, looked at her a moment then flew right up and delicately touched her on the beak – a bird's kiss – flying back to his perch directly afterwards. She leant forward to receive the touch, carefully wiping her beak on the branch as soon as his back was turned. She then flew to a tree farther off from her mate, he followed to perch opposite, as before flying up in graceful manner to touch her bill, held out to him. For half an hour I watched them go from tree to tree, where always in the same way this one gentle touch on the beak was given and received without more bill-wiping from her in the intervals.

Later they flew to their last year's nesting site, a tall, thick bush in my neighbour's orchard.

March 25th. Progress seems to be made in Chanter's wooing. He and his mate were this morning perched a foot apart on the bough of a tree and he kept dancing up to her with quick eager movements, now giving her several billings each time. She was perched with her back to him, but always turned her head towards him for the billings. Later they fed on their old nesting-tree where now they are often seen. Chanter stretched out his head to peck a budding leaf on a twig almost out of reach, lost his balance and tumbled over, landing lower down on the bush. Completely unconcerned, he continued feeding from another twig above him as if the fall had been intentional. I have several times seen Bullfinches lose their balance and fall in disorderly manner to lower branches when trying to peck buds out of their reach.

On the days following the above notes, Chanter and his mate were always seen in close company; if she lost sight of him for a moment his piping notes quickly led her to him. The charming tune of his full song is recorded in Bird Song Chapter 12. Although the whole tune was not often sung, he frequently piped the opening notes or the cadence, the soft tones of his voice and dignity of his plain song in keeping with the character of the gentle-mannered Bullfinch.

When Chanter's young were fledged these quaint babies, with stout little bodies and as yet scarcely any tail, were brought to my garden, the parents spending much time on the flower-beds, extracting seeds from forget-me-nots which were fed to the fledglings, who perched in a row on the pergola. Chanter and his mate also were often to be seen clinging to cow-parsley, arched under their weight while they plucked the ripening seeds. Their young, calling softly and persistently, fluttered round them when hunger made them impatient; often they attempted to alight on thin stems of long grasses or wild flowers that would not hold their weight, many swaying perches being tried before they found one where they could settle with closed wings.

I think the damage Bullfinches do to fruit-buds has been exaggerated, for it is a fact my trees bear crops equal to those in orchards where no Bullfinches feed. In early spring these birds take mostly green salad in the form of leaf-buds, this thinning of leaves seeming to improve the quantity of flower-buds. When blossoming starts they first choose wild plums and crab apples that grow in the hedges of my orchard, then they work at pear and apple-trees, particularly the former, yet all these trees are heavily laden with fruit each year (except an occasional miss when the tree is resting). I have come to the conclusion the Bull-finch must only take diseased buds. The only time noticeable damage has been done was one year when a mischievous Bullfinch nipped off every flower from three artificial crabs, the ground beneath becoming white as snow, but the sight of this beautiful bird in the blossom well repaid the early loss of bloom. This year my cherry crab-apples bore much fruit (as well as all the other fruit-trees in the orchard), and these decorative bright-red little apples were sought by Blackbirds, Thrushes, Robins and two Blackcaps. The latter spent five days in the last week of September feeding almost continuously on this fruit, before leaving on their journey. A more charming bird picture cannot be imagined than these Blackcaps, male and female, bending their dark, glossy heads over the little red apples that glowed like miniature Chinese lanterns and often swung to and fro at the first touch of their beaks if they pecked the sides without holding the apples, for they hang on long stems. The Blackcaps watched intently until the swing-ing ceased then gave another sharper stab, finding this made more swinging, they ended by perching where they could attack the crab from above, steadying the stem at the same time. When the apples were hollowed to the core the Chaffinches had their turn, for their chosen portion of fruit is always the pips.

CHAFFINCH

At one time I had several Chaffinches who took, or rather snatched, food from my hand. Once they discovered food could be got in this way their demands became persistent and they were so boisterous over their snatchings, flying up like whirlwinds while shouting shrill call-notes, that they created a commotion which upset the Tits, who perch in friendly manner and were continually being swept off my hand. The result was that the Tits started quick snatchings, merely to avoid the Chaffinches, so I had to give up encouraging hand-tame Chaf-finches excepting one called Chink, whom I have now had constantly in my garden for nine years. He flies down straight from the trees at my call of 'Chink, Chink,' in a voice made as sharp as possible. But he, like the others, snatches the food, taking three or four pieces if possible, though dropping some as he flies away. He has never perched to eat on my hand like the Tits, Robins and some Blackbirds. Chink only comes for food and unlike the other species, shows little interest in my company. He appears not to have the intelligence to find his way in and out of the windows to get food, however hungry he may be, but he flies to meet me along roads with the Tits and follows after me a little way when I go out in winter-time. Early in spring his demands become exorbitant. If I am sitting in the garden he perches on the back of my chair and shouts call-notes and song right into my ear until more food is forthcoming; if I refuse to pay attention he persistently calls until I grow deafened by the loud, shrill tones close to the drum of my ear, so when I have no more food I offer him a leaf to every few call-notes, which displeases him, his expression looks bored and at about the tenth leaf he darts off at great speed, as if to make up for lost time. He then starts chasing his mate or intruding birds, leaving me in peace to watch and admire the slick cut of a Chaffinch's flight.

Chink's nesting territory varies between the orchard and front garden. All the year round he stays with me, but his mate and the other females, who nested or were bred in the garden, leave in the autumn except for occasional return visits. Some of the young males bred in the garden remain for the autumn, or even until early spring, although they are away some days, when I presume they join flocks. I generally see more females than males in my garden in early spring, some I recognise as the returned females who nested the previous year or the young reared the previous summer. But some are, I think, strangers to my garden.

Chink kept to the same mate for six years, although he must have had plenty of choice with all these females around, apparently anxious to stay in his territory where some of them had been bred. His mate was very tame and followed me about but she would not come to my hand and every time I threw her food in the presence of Chink, he snatched it from her and hurriedly ate it himself. I never saw him feed her or stand aside for her to take food she was given. Another couple of Chaffinches, whose nest was on a bare branch just above where I habitually sit in the orchard, were also very tame, and I had good chances of close observation. The male never fed his mate while sitting or when off the nest, but like Chink, he fed the young attentively. Another pair that I was less familiar with and only occasionally watched, had a nest high up in a hedge. This male seemed often to feed his mate while sitting, for if I watched a short while he was sure to appear and fly to the nest with food. (*The Handbook of British Birds* states male Chaffinches feed females while sitting. From my observations it seems according to the individual.) The mate of the former bird bound the moss of her nest with long strands of sewing cotton stolen from me. She found for herself the method we use when carrying a long rope; she looped it into a coil, first picking up one end then taking up the rest of the yard-long strand at two-inch intervals until she had it all neatly coiled in her bill. Carrying the cotton uncoiled it would get entangled in twigs surrounding her nest, so be difficult to use.

One year Chink's mate built her nest on my pergola. The nestlings were amusing to watch when nearly ready to fly. The neat little nest being too small for the fat-looking babies, they bulged over the rim and kept standing on each other's backs to stretch or preen. One morning four flew boldly from the nest, following quickly after each other without a moment's hesitation, and landing in trees across the lawn; but one was left behind, afraid to take the plunge. It stood on the rim of the nest, giving an interesting study of quick-changing poses and facial expressions. First upright with outstretched head looking for the others, then crouching low, its face contorted with fear. After a moment it began to preen, looked comfortable and fluffed out its feathers, a fat, contented babyish expression on its face, next moment it drew itself up to full height, raised its wings slightly, looked upwards, then sank down on the rim of the nest, misery in its attitude and on its face. The parents kept away from the nest; they had not been near when the others flew. At last the lone fledgling stood bolt upright and with a confident expression fluttered its wings and was off on a long flight, terminating inside a bedroom in my neighbour's house. Chink followed directly afterwards, the window was wide open at the bottom and he hovered on the sill, calling in gentle tones or fluttering in front of the window until at last the fledgling flew out to the sill and was fed. Afterwards it perched on a creeper by the window, apparently

afraid to risk another flight. It was not the smallest of the brood and it
was very strong on the wing for a fledgling, but in temperament it was
nervous and for some days it remained apart from the others, clinging
to the wall creeper or nearby tree. The nervous baby bird does not
only fear flight but the difficulty of landing on a perch has to be overcome. I think this baby flew on and on, past bushes and trees into the
bedroom, because it could not face alighting once it was on the wing.
I have seen other newly-fledged young of various species wanting to
follow after the rest of the brood, but obviously having too much
difficulty over judging where to perch and how to do it. Even hopping from short distances to perch on my hand causes fledglings
some trouble. They are not afraid of my hand, for they are tame and
fearless of me, but it is a question of measuring the distance accurately and knowing what to do with their legs. They often alight
more awkwardly from a short distance of about a foot than from
farther off.

Expressions of fledgling birds in all species are fascinating to watch.
A baby Green Woodpecker came last summer to my garden for two
days. It was plump and flufly and kept looking for parents who were
slow to come; its poses of expectancy and sudden relapses into a bored
stare when the supposed parent turned out to be a Starling or Blackbird were suitable for filming. I made the following notes:

June 18th. A fledgling Green Woodpecker close to my cottage resting in a fork against the tree-bole, feathers fluffed out, looking rotund
in shape instead of the characteristic long bodied Woodpecker appearance. It frequently called for food but no parent came. After an hour it
suddenly held erect its head and called 'pee, pee, pee, pee, pee,' in a
high-pitched voice, its pose the pleading baby with helplessness in its
attitude. Then 'Yik, Yik,' loudly and peremptorily, its pose now very
expectant, with neck fully stretched out and head craning forward,
eyes goggling with excitement. For that moment it became long-
shaped like an adult, although its tail was so short. Then it suddenly
subsided into fat fluffiness again, its face dejected, for the expected
parent had passed across the garden, but would not feed the fledgling
where it was perched. Next moment the baby flew to the orchard, its
flight slow but the wings flapping at a quick pace. It did not dip, with
closed wings, like the adult Woodpecker. Very young fledglings in all
species make a vigorous effort of continuous fast wing-flappings; only

when experienced do they adopt the alternate closing and beating of wings in flight, making the dip which is habitual to many passerines.

GREENFINCH

My first year in Bird Cottage, when hemp-seed and peanuts were easily obtainable in unlimited supply for about fourpence a pound, I was able to attract and tame more species than has since been possible. Greenfinches, as well as many others, have a passion for hemp-seed, and they were amusing to watch when I could supply this on the bird-table. While the parents perched on the hemp-bowl, eating large quantities, their young used to climb on their backs, calling noisily and impatiently, pushing each other off and taking turns to scramble up with much wing-fluttering. The parents stolidly continued eating as if unconscious of their chattering fledglings who tumbled about on their backs. Then suddenly the whole family flew to another perch, where the clamorous young were fed.

In winter one particular Greenfinch installed himself as owner of the hemp. When the Judge (so called because of his expression) had eaten his fill he continued to sit on the small seed-container, preventing any other bird from taking its share. One after another the hungry birds attempted to snatch a seed, trying many dodges, particularly attacks from behind, but the Judge always swung round and faced the other bird. There was much excitable display from the attacker, but the Judge was calm, he merely thrust forward his head and snapped his strong beak several times at the heads of the hungry birds. They were nervous of him and never could shift him from his seat on the container. At his own time he flew off, perhaps to stretch his wings and get up another appetite, for he was generally back again before long. The moment he left the hemp-bowl it was surrounded by a dozen birds, Greenfinches, Sparrows, Chaffinches, all jostling each other in eagerness to seize some grains of seed, but the Great Tits, who also love hemp-seed, kept aloof until the mob had dispersed. Sometimes I pushed the Judge off the container, both for the good of his soul and because of the hungry birds. If the container was empty the Judge sat on the window-sill, his beak pressed against the glass, watching my movements inside the room with embarrassing intentness; every few moments he gave one small tap on the pane, his persistent concentrated gaze and quiet, determined tapping impossible to ignore. So after a while he got what he wanted and it caused me much distress when the Judge tapped in vain, for I could no longer buy the seed. He then withdrew from the bird-table, as did all other Greenfinches. Since then I have had no intimacy with this species, although they nest in my garden and feed on the anchusas, growing under my windows, when the seeds are ripe.

GOLDFINCH

All round my cottage I have grown teazels for the Goldfinches. Sometimes twenty of these birds have been perched on them, extracting the seeds. In summer and autumn my garden is enlivened by a continuous trickle of their family chatter as the young flutter over flower-beds while the parents are gathering seeds of various plants, corn-flower and michaelmas daisies in their season being a favourite choice.

When extracting seeds from teazels they make a curious buzzing sound, suggesting a zither accompaniment to their musical twittering while they feed. A vibratory movement of the head when the beak is inserted into the seed-pocket seems necessary before the seeds can be pulled out, unless they are very ripe. This produces the buzzing, which carries a long distance, like the Woodpecker's drumming. I recently watched some young Goldfinches try unsuccessfully to extract seeds without the vibratory movement. Puzzled at their failure, they kept watching their parents' neat action but could not copy the vibratory trick and only moved their heads from side to side in the teazel pockets. This accomplished nothing, it made no sound, also failed to entice the seed out, although they got their beaks well into the pockets. It was amusing to watch the puzzled expressions of the young birds, who kept turning to look at their parents then trying to imitate the actions. It reminded me of beginners at the violin who attempt to make vibrato, but the fingers will not vibrate. How the accomplished teazel performer made such a loud buzzing that carried so far at first puzzled me, but undoubtedly vibratory beak action on stiff surface has the effect of producing life and strength to the sound just as the violinist's tone gains life through use of vibrato, which intensifies vibrations and brings more natural harmonics into play.

My Goldfinches always nest high up in evergreen trees, where little can be seen of their nesting affairs. A friend once brought me a nestling picked up in the road of a country town. It was only a few days old, still in down with half-open eyes, but black and gold was just beginning to show on its wings. The vitality of this immature bird was astonishing. When I put it into an improvised nest it scrambled out again and came towards me across the room to climb into the palm of my outstretched hand, there snuggling down to sleep. I fed it every hour during daylight on bread and milk, but the second day it shut its beak tight when I tried to give it this unnatural food, which disagreed with its digestion. No bird-seed of a suitable kind was then available. There were many Goldfinches in the garden and the nestling stretched up its head and cried at the sound of their voices, so I put the improvised nest on top of a hedge, leaving the nestling for an hour in the hope that some parent Goldfinch would hear its cries and, like Baldhead and his mate, adopt the orphan. When I returned the nestling had disappeared, nor was it to be found anywhere near the hedge.

SPARROWS AND SWALLOWS

Because Sparrows, with their ill-mannered, pushful ways drive other birds away, I keep them at a distance as far as possible, but there are always numbers of House- and Tree-Sparrows around my hedges. Perhaps because of this, Swallows or House-Martins do not build near my cottage. When, in late summer, a few perch with their young on the wires over my garden, often these rude Sparrows drive them off by flying up and squawking scold-notes close to their ears, much to my annoyance, for there are no birds more beautiful to study at close quarters. Last autumn a family of full-grown young Swallows were perched on the rails of some steps and when I walked up to them, putting my hand on the rails, they did not fly away but looked up into my face, as if inquisitively, then seemed to forget my presence altogether although the nearest one was within an inch of my hand. I shall never forget the lovely look in its eyes, wild and intent yet with a far-seeing expression that was indescribably touching, as was the beauty of its fresh young

plumage. The sheen in the sunlight of its dark blue wings and wonderfully soft-looking breast-feathers tinged with a faint flush, the
lovely-shaped head and glowing, deep-toned colours all made such a
setting for those expressive eyes. One of the great joys of close and
intimate bird-watching is learning the expressions in their eyes, also
seeing the texture and colours of plumage, the reflections of light on
their feathers giving an infinite variety of shades in colour to each
bird.*

THRUSH

I find it difficult to study the Thrush intimately chiefly because the
Blackbirds push them into the background. The latter become possessive when encouraged to tameness and the Thrushes, who seem
nervous of their big, black relation, allow themselves to be chased
away unless they are very hungry. But sometimes they find ways of
dodging the chaser. I have one Thrush who gets the better of Darky,
the Blackbird, by darting up from behind, sweeping round him and
seizing food so quickly that Darky's heavier chasing movement misses
fire; he turns first in one direction then the other and ends by tilting up
his head with a queer expression in the direction of the departed
Thrush, who by nature is slow in movement when seeking food, but
can learn to outwit his troublesome relation by bringing into play the
quick action of which he is capable.

Last summer when food was very scarce for Thrush tribes owing to
prolonged drought, my Blackbirds relaxed possessiveness and let all
Thrushes take food without molestation. Then it was the Thrushes
who went for each other, heads lowered to the ground, bills snapping
and backs raised in the attitude of combat. Neighbouring parent birds
who needed food for their young boldly defied the residents and much
sparring occurred. When the two young of one brood were old

---

* There are two kinds of colour in birds' feathers, namely, pigmentation and
structural, the latter arising from the splitting up of the white light at the fine
feather structure. The surface of minute air bubbles inside the tiny barbules of the
feathers splits up the light, giving rainbow reflections like oil does on the surface
of water.

enough to fend for themselves they used to wait by the kitchen door while calling me in sharp clicking notes until I fed them. The young of my resident Thrush went to the front of the cottage and were fed by the bird-table, while another youngster called me to feed it on the orchard side of the cottage. The parent birds sought me and were fed wherever I happened to be, perhaps at the top of the orchard or down the garden, but the young ones always called me to them in their chosen places, thus settling their own disputes – for the residents still chased the young of neighbours if they came into contact. The young Blackbirds used to follow me wherever I went, like their parents, for Blackbirds seem to relax territorial behaviour during drought or other times of need.

SPOTTED FLYCATCHER

One year a Spotted Flycatcher nested outside my window, between the top of some trellis-work and the wall. The male took no practical share in the building, but he fed her frequently at the nest while she was working. I made these notes at the time. – The Spotted Flycatcher is very agile over her building, she collects much of her material on the wing, pulling at cobwebs while hovering on fluttering wings before tree branches and fences, her flight quick and soft as she returns to her nest. She also binds the moss to the trellis-work with coloured cotton strands – gathered from my chair after I have taken tackings from sewing. She has to hold her wings and tail straight upwards in order to turn round while moulding her nest in this narrow site. Her mate often flies up while she is working, hovering close to the nest as if to watch its progress and encourage her with many softly-warbled notes, quietly and hurriedly sung. When he presents her with flies they twitter together in a charming manner after each fly is swallowed. He warbles in a Martin-like way at times, this song very sweet and soft, so different from the emphatic notes more frequently heard . . . The Spotted Flycatcher and Dobs, my Robin, have just been rolling together on the ground at my feet. The Flycatchers seem to feel the cottage is theirs now she is sitting on her nest beside the french window. Not only am I reprimanded when entering this window, but she attacks the Tits, Robin or any other bird who flies through the front windows; she darts from her nest to fly fiercely at us with half-hissed, half-whispered swear-notes! It is an awkward situation, this newcomer taking possession and my old friends driven away! Fighting sometimes follows, my residents giving way after a short tussle, for nesting sites have to be respected. My Tits have the sense to enter mostly by side windows, but Dobs, with slower wits, never thinks of doing this. The Flycatcher sits restlessly, her white chin always craned up as she looks for her mate or watches what goes on within her view. Every movement of mine she follows, her head turning about and eyes intently gazing as if with the interest of a bird-watcher! I feel she gives back in good measure the staring I have done while she built her nest.

Before the Flycatcher's eggs were hatched I went away from home for a fortnight. On my return she was sitting on another clutch, her nest now on trellis-work against the back wall of my cottage instead of the front. Her first nest had been robbed; it lay in two pieces on the ground. Anxious lest the robber should return, I kept close watch over her nest. This time the Flycatchers did not once fly at me with hisses of disapproval even when I arranged wire netting round the nest. It seemed, by their altered friendly manner, that they understood I was giving them protection, which luckily proved a success. The family were a delight to watch, for baby Flycatchers have much charm.

When the time came for fledging, as with Chink's young, four made bold flights but one was left behind in the nest, too afraid for flight, its sensitive face even more expressive of changing emotions than the baby Chaffinch's. Often in overcoming fears courage is developed. Perhaps this may apply to the baby bird's first struggle against fear of leaving the nest and trusting to untried wings. I watched this struggle working in the baby Flycatcher, clinging alone to its nest after the others had flown; the terrified distortions of its face in the effort to overcome fear and the sublime moment of standing up, wings opened and no trace of fear left on its face – trusting at last. It was a miniature heaven from hell and a grand sight.

CHAPTER 8

The Mind of a Bird

When trying to form some estimation of the mind of a bird it must be realised that there is an immense amount of difference in the character and intelligence of individuals both within and between the species.

Examining the physical structure of a bird's brain it is found that the corpus striatum – connected with emotional activity – is very highly developed, with relatively many fibres compared to man, but the cortex of the brain is not so highly developed. This might be expected since birds' emotions are much in evidence, a lesser amount of intelligence being shown.

They are very sensitive and highly keyed, with quicker pulses and warmer blood than man. Added to their keen sight and hearing, they have a well-developed sense of direction, necessary because of their powers of flight, also probably some other senses which are undeveloped in man.

EMOTIONS

Fear

Fear and suspicion of their enemy man, who so often harms and tortures birds, naturally plays a large part in their life. They are always alert for danger when the human who has not gained their complete confidence is in sight, so it is hard for us to watch their behaviour intimately, which is necessary for a fuller understanding of their minds. At the slightest suspicion of fear a bird entirely alters its natural behaviour; it becomes hesitant, its actions cautious and guarded, this often creating false impressions about the bird.

Some are by nature far more nervous than others, it is a question of temperament. This was seen in the fledging incidents related in the last chapter. Often those who are most timid when very young prove the most intelligent and interesting characters; being more sensitive, they are more responsive once fear of the human is overcome. The Great Tit Curley was an example of this.

Nestlings seem free of all fears until parents have taught them to crouch at warning notes or they have had some frightening experience, in which case they afterwards crouch at any unfamiliar object moving above or near their nest. So many hazards beset a bird and discrimination must be used to decide which are dangerous, which can be ignored, and this the young bird gradually learns after leaving the nest, from watching other birds and from warning notes. Their parents teach them to keep off the ground and under cover from above. The temperamentally nervous fledglings cautiously keep to safe perches, but there are bold ones whose interest in the world around them at times makes them disregard safety precautions. If one of these continues to make itself conspicuous by chattering or moving about after a warning note that a cat is near (ground danger warning is generally different from an air warning), the parent may give a subdued scold-note accompanied by a tap on the head with its beak. This immediately silences the youngster; if a nestling, it crouches, if a fledgling, it stays rigid upon its perch until it sees from other birds that danger is over. If the warning note to take cover from above is unheeded, the parent Great Tit sometimes pushes the fledgling from its exposed perch by kicking from above with its feet, scold-notes accompanying the push.

Once the young have witnessed the terrifying sight of a fledgling being carried off by a Jackdaw, cat, or bird of prey, they become excessively cautious, taking fright unnecessarily many times a day. If nestlings, they crouch at every movement above or near their nest; if fledglings, they rush to shelter with sharp cries of alarm, though the supposed dangers may be such things as the neighbouring Blackbird swooping down to steal food from another's territory or a Swallow sweeping low overhead. Anything suddenly passing near them causes alarm, for they have not yet learnt to distinguish what is harmful to them. Especially they fear aeroplanes at this stage, even the sound of one is recognised without seeing it approach. Sometimes when a fledgling Great Tit is in rigid pose, freezing at the sound of a distant plane, its parent arrives with food, and although the parent keeps pushing the caterpillar against the closed beak of its frozen offspring the food is ignored and the fledgling keeps rigid on its perch while looking upwards with the blinking eyes that denote fear. At last it relaxes enough to take food, but stays motionless upon its perch until all sound of the plane has died away. By degrees they learn the real dangers, their terror of planes or sweeping Swallows is first reduced to a suspicious stare then gradually these are disregarded altogether – although the roar of a plane very close overhead always alarms my birds.

Their ears as well as their eyes are alert for enemies and they connect sound and sight of anything suspicious even from the first time of appearance. They also learn to distinguish between the dangerous Jackdaw seeking prey and the one flying overhead for other purposes – perhaps the tense pose of head being the danger signal, for I can judge by this myself.

Birds have numerous ways of showing their fears. It is only in acute fear the posture is rigid. Frequent head-turning of a certain kind denotes suspicion, but familiarity with the individual is often necessary before all the nervous mannerisms and fear reactions are recognised as such.

Parent birds are always alert for possible danger to their young, but cease at this period to heed danger to themselves. It is noticeable how much more intense their suffering seems when afraid for their young than when fear is on their own account. Mortality among very young chicks is appallingly high, so their difficulty in rearing a brood with so many creatures against them – man included – would account for the extreme fear of parent birds.

When birds take cover at warning notes which prove false alarms, from watching the expression in their eyes and their rapid recovery to normal behaviour, it is evident fear is only felt momentarily; if danger has been real, a hawk flying overhead, etc., then complete recovery from fright takes a few minutes, even after the danger has passed.

State of health affects fear; in moult, illness or any disability they generally become painfully nervous for their weakened physique makes them lose confidence in themselves.

The courage birds show through the dangers and difficulties of their life is immense, especially when protecting their young – their bravery the greater because they are sensitive and alive to danger. Some show more courage than others, for, as in all things, it rests much with the individual.

General Emotions

Many ornithologists at the present time say that bird and human mind are completely different, and that the former have not such emotions as love, hatred, jealousy, etc., clearly defined. It is thought they react automatically in set patterns of behaviour according to the stimulus. Details of such theories will be known to the readers of recent literature on this subject, but I wish in the following pages of this chapter to give reasons why I think that this view is inadequate to explain the nature and behaviour of birds.

It is probable I shall be accused of some anthropomorphism in the bird biographies and other accounts in this book, but all my descriptions of how the birds behaved are strictly accurate although it is difficult to give detailed narratives of bird behaviour in natural language without a little anthropomorphism. If a specialised ornithological vocabulary existed, full enough for describing their ways, it would sound less anthropomorphic, but it would then be as unintelligible to the ordinary reader as a lawyer's document! Besides this, after the incidents I have witnessed during eleven years of observation of individual birds at close quarters, I cannot think that their mind is so remote from ours. It seems reasonable to think that they have some resemblances although, of course, many differences. I should like to stress the point that birds have a language for their needs, they have recreations, even taking the form of definite games something like ours, they have developed song and use it as a means of expression. In some cases their music is akin to ours (see Blackbirds in Chapter 11).

All my evidence is from watching individual birds at close quarters when they are free. With patience it is possible in this way to learn much from the expression in their eyes, and inflections of movement and of voice which together form their language. For instance, in the gaping displays common among many species of birds, there are inflections of gape that, together with eye expression, give different meanings to the gape. With birds that I know intimately, the meanings of their various gapes is apparent to me, because I know their expressions and understand the small inflections in their manner of gaping, this being in many cases essential for correct interpretation. There is often a faint, almost inaudible sound, only heard when very close, or there may be a loud hiss in the case of a threatening or angry

Great Tit choosing a shell.
September 1950.

The shell game interrupted as the
camera flashes. *September 1950.*

Great Tit, looking to see if anyone is occupying his roost-box
and entering his roost. *July 1950.*

Great Tits, young and adult, like getting at books. *September 1950.*

A young Cuckoo brought to me while Eric Hosking was photographing my birds. It was injured and died that night. Its skin has been preserved in the British Natural History Museum, South Kensington. *July 1950.*

Spotted Flycatcher.

Spotted Flycatcher hovering before nest.

Parcels are always examined and torn open by Great Tits. These are two adult males. *September 1950.*

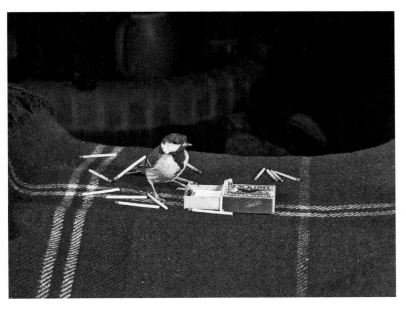

Great Tit throwing matches. *September 1950.*

Great Tits in their nest.

Willow-Warbler singing.

Sedge-Warbler

Nightingale.

The same bird in an aggressive display.

Sky-Lark

Song Thrush

gape, with blazing eyes. The beak, in spite of its hard texture, quickly shows emotion, for it has subtle variations of movement and these movements can be read when intimate with a bird – as with humans we get to know and read the expressions of their mouth. Birds, when wanting something, often give slow gapes; if it is food they want the beak may also be quickly opened and shut, perhaps several times. They may make the same kind of slow gape with a different eye expression and posture when suddenly warm sunshine is felt on their feathers, suggesting sunbathing to them. If quite close to the bird a very slight wing-twitch will also be seen, then if circumstances are favourable the bird retreats to a suitable spot for spreading wings and tail feathers to sunbathe. An amusing gape to watch is the one sometimes given when a bird is suddenly frustrated by another bird forestalling him unexpectedly. A faint sound generally is made, like a suppressed exclamation, and the eyes have a comical expression, for a mixture of emotions cause this gape. The bird has been surprised and thwarted, momentarily he seems undecided how to act; he may be left gaping with this queer expression and a hesitant pose while his forestaller gets off scathless. Another gape that seems really a grimace is made by Great Tits when they are expecting a nut and are given something less to their taste. The beak is half-opened and a faint sound made, resembling air coming out of a bottle when uncorking it. The whole expression is one of disgust. There is, of course, the well-known gaping accompanied by baby-cry imitations, used by the adult at certain periods of nesting season. In all these cases and many more, the emotion can be identified by the eye expressions and different inflections and manner of gaping. The same applies to all other forms of display.

The intimate knowledge of a bird needed before a correct interpretation of its behaviour can be given is evidenced by the following instances.

1. The Blackbird, Oakleaf, picks up a leaf to go into battle. He runs across the lawn, disappearing behind bushes, the oak-leaf held in his bill. The bird-watcher unfamiliar with this Blackbird might well think the male bird was participating in nest-building; but Oakleaf carries leaves for purposes entirely his own. (See Chapter 3, Part 2.) He also has occasionally been seen to hold up a leaf before his mate when

wooing, but from the different facial expression and manner of displaying it I know which purpose is meant by his action. If the human who is intimate with the bird can distinguish subtle differences in similar actions or displays how much more apparent these distinctions would appear to their own species or race.

2. One Great Tit used to ask for food, as I first thought, by the incongruous action of a persistent flea-hunt in his breast-feathers. Birds have various ways of asking for food, but this extraordinary display gave an impression the bird was half-witted. After fixing his eyes on me intently for a moment, he bent his head down and hurriedly poked his beak in and out of his breast-feathers like a dog snapping at fleas. The action was curiously jerky and never used when preening. At intervals he stopped to fix his eyes on me with a pleading expression, then the flea-hunt was resumed. When this bird got to know me well this curious performance ceased. It was only a nervous habit brought out by shyness in asking for food. This bird was Whiskers, Curley's mate, and he again showed this nervous habit when Curley could not lay eggs and he was growing impatient. Birds are very prone to contract nervous habits which can easily be misconstrued, this often creating a false impression of stupidity or indefinite emotion.

3. An instance occurred recently that appeared like parental stupidity and lack of recognition, but proved to be the reverse. A brood of Great Tits had flown in the. morning, all except the smallest who clambered from the nest, clung to the bole of the tree and fell to the ground. The parents tried to coax it up again, but its wings had not strength to fly upwards. It found a secluded spot under the low sheltering branch of a very young lawsonia tree. Long grass around it gave some protection, but I was afraid of neighbours' cats who devour many of my garden fledglings. So towards evening I placed the baby bird on a wide branch of another small tree nearby, being afraid to move it far away in case the parents had difficulty in finding it. Soon the father bird came with food and although the fledgling cried lustily the father only gave one glance at his offspring, then agitatedly hopped around under the first tree as if concerned about the fledgling's disappearance. He then flew to the tree where it was perched, crying for food, but immediately returned to the ground under the other tree and, looking up at me, gave several scold-notes. I understood the meaning of his behaviour at last; where I had placed the fledgling was

exposed from above and it would be easy prey for the Jackdaws and Magpies who pick off many young from my garden, so it was safer on the ground under cover of the other tree. A parent bird will not feed its young on a dangerous perch because this entices it to remain there instead of seeking safer cover or following after its parent. While the father bird flew off to feed his other fledglings, I took the small one right across the garden and placed it on the branch of a tree that had very dense foliage. The fledgling was now concealed from above and below, but far off from its original spot under the lawsonia near its nest, so this would be a test of recognition. It continued to cry and next minute the father bird flew up in a pleased manner, fed the baby without hesitation and gave two or three gentle notes (the usual soft notes given when the young first fly). Then he flew to the tree-top and gave loud call-notes to which the mother bird responded. She came hurrying to the tree and together they flew to their youngest fledgling, obviously delighted that it was at last on a safe perch. They fed it several times then displayed together excitedly on the bough beside the fledgling, in a manner usual when all have flown from the nest. If I had not understood the father bird's behaviour and the reason for his scold-notes when he refused to feed the baby in response to its cries when on that exposed perch, it would have appeared like a case of lack of recognition of his own young, whereas it was an example of sensible behaviour. My birds can make me understand by their notes and actions or inflections of movement what is passing through their minds. If I do not get their meaning at once they soon find a way of communication, often acting like in a dumb charade, which is a way frequently used among themselves for explaining what they want.

There is much variation over display with species and with individuals, some displaying far more than others, the intelligent species varying most.

Some of the reasons given for thinking birds have not our clearly-defined emotions is that their displays – including gaping – do not seem to have any single identifiable emotion, that in some species threat and sexual display is alike, in some distinct, and that they are able to switch suddenly from one emotion to another and back again according to the other individual's response. But the human being is just as indefinite if we judge from outward display. Some races and individuals blush, gesticulate, or make other manifestations of emotion much more than others, but the extent of their feelings cannot be assessed by these outward signs. It may be the same with birds.

Threat and sexual display would not seem alike to the birds themselves because of the different inflections of movement, etc., that act as a language, some of which even the bird-watcher can understand if intimate with the individual. But probably there are many details in display which have significance to the birds, which no human could possibly follow or understand.

Time goes at a different pace to birds, they have faster pulses, higher temperatures, their sight and hearing quicker and their actions often at a pace we cannot follow with our eyes. Their reactions would not seem quick-changing to them, and it is natural their spontaneous natures would react instantaneously according to the behaviour of their associates. So these quick-seeming changes are no proof of indefinite feelings.

Their emotions may be clearly defined when the action seems inappropriate, for instance, when the bird sings from shock. It has been stated a bird is incapable of love, or heartless, because he may sing when his mate is killed even before the warmth has left her body. When this happens it is because his emotions are violently stirred and he must give them outlet. I have known birds sing loudly directly their mates have been run over by traffic outside my gate. When this outburst of agitated song is over they will appear to be moping at their loss, and cease singing altogether for several days. The reaction depends upon the individual, some recovering sooner than others, perhaps because there is much more attachment between some mates.

So that from all one witnesses of bird behaviour, there seems no reason for assuming they have not these simple emotions clearly defined.

MEMORY AND RECOGNITION

I find birds remember each other when they meet at my house after several months separation during nesting season. There are some who have special antipathy for another of their species, and this is always shown in exactly the same individual manner. For instance, Curley and Twist were apart for three months each nesting season yet, when meeting again, their antagonism, which was noticeable as fledglings, was always shown in the same ways; but they were not antagonistic to others of their species. (Chapter 2, Part 4.) Similarly, Baldhead became intolerant of Fatty after the unusual nesting affairs related in Chapter 2, Part 2, his intolerance being shown after each period of Fatty's absence from the cottage. There are some birds who are especially friendly towards each other, and this same immediate recognition applies. Strangers are tolerated or not, according to circumstances and individuals. Even in the distance, recognition and remembrance of each other is shown by their different reactions, without a note having been uttered. They distinguish me from other humans across two or three large fields, even in clothes they have never before seen me wear. (See page 76.)

They have no difficulty in distinguishing their own fledglings from those of others, for in my garden it often happens the young from one nest stray near the nest of another brood, the same species and age. The trespassing fledglings are driven away at once by scold-notes if very close to the strangers' nest – unless circumstances are unusual as in Baldhead's adoption of the orphans.

As before mentioned, one Great Tit recognised me after two years' absence, and various other tests show that my garden birds remember me after several months' absence, Tits, Robins, Blackbirds, Chaffinches coming straight to my hand, although some may flutter round me hesitatingly just at first even after a week's separation. It depends upon the individual. (See Chapter 5.)

INTELLIGENCE

Because, at the present time, it seems the tendency is to underestimate bird intelligence, I am purposely giving most attention to this subject in writing of bird mind, choosing an intelligent species for many examples.

1. The Great Tit Jane, whose biography is given in Chapter 2, showed much agitation the first time her fledglings flew close to the windows of my cottage. Young birds often bang against glass, accidents occurring if they enter a room before understanding window-panes – for the fledgling easily succumbs if its head is hit, the older bird being able to stand a much harder blow. Jane must have realised the danger

of glass for, after a few moments of agitated fluttering over her fledglings, she seized some food, called her young to the open fanlight – where there is a perch for birds – then quickly placed herself so that she could hold the food to her young with the glass intervening. They tried to get it and, of course, pecked the glass. She next put her head outside the window to show the food to her fledglings without the glass barrier, but before they could take it she withdrew behind the window-pane and held it so they pecked the glass again. She repeated this three times; by then her young, with characteristic quickness of Great Tits, had understood and were examining the window-panes with quaint expressions of interest on their faces. There was no trouble when they afterwards followed their parents into the room because Jane had taught them to know glass; they were cautious when approaching the windows, found their way out of the open ones and never banged into those that were closed. What else except reasoning power could have accounted for Jane's action?

Parent birds teach their young many things. Although some of their lessons are simple compared to the above, teaching, even in its simplest form, is beyond the field of automatic behaviour. That a bird has the perception to foresee the necessity of teaching her young to know glass, shows that reasoning enters into their intelligence and that this is of a higher order than is generally supposed.

2. One December day a Blue Tit, new to my cottage, flew into the room through the small fanlight which in winter is usually the only open window. It tried to get out again by a closed one on the opposite side of the room, fluttering and banging itself against the pane in panic-stricken efforts. Another Blue Tit, familiar with my room and the fanlight, saw from outside the closed window this frightened Tit struggling against the panes. After watching a moment with a worried expression,[*] the outside Tit flew hurriedly round to the other side of the cottage, entered through the fanlight, paused a second on the sill to call gently, but finding no notice was taken the rescuer flew across the room and touched the fluttering Tit, who immediately turned round to follow the rescuer back across the room and out of the narrowly-opened fanlight. In going to fetch the stranger-Tit the rescuer showed thought amounting to reasoning power. The less intelligent bird tries to contact the frightened one inside by flying to the outside of the window-pane, this happening sometimes in similar

cases. Great Tits also occasionally help each other to find their way out of the fanlight in much the same way as did the Blue Tit. Being highly nervous, excitable birds, the stranger Great Tit flies wildly from window to window, banging into the panes with such force it may be half-stunned on a sill by the time its rescuer arrives, sometimes clinging to the curtain and gazing with a worried expression* at the gasping, half-stunned Tit. When the latter shows signs of recovering the rescuer may have to fly backwards and forwards from the fanlight to the sill several times before it quite recovers consciousness, then the two birds fly through the fanlight, the stranger following with a deliberate flight quite different from the panic-stricken plunges it had made without the guidance of a rescuer.

I am continually seeing birds faced with situations new to them and it has been my experience to find that unless they are paralysed with fright they act intelligently, the degree varying according to the individual as well as the species.

Birds have applied their brains to the craft of nest-building with wonderful skill and although we loosely say that they build by instinct, this does not cover many of the things that go to the building of a nest. They have to overcome such difficulties as the following:

One of my Great Tits, Smoke, this year chose a large petrol tin for her nest. It being hung aslant, she skidded on the slippery surface when she took in her first bits of moss, so she began bringing some small sticks for a foundation. This is unusual for Tits; they choose moss, wool or other flexible material easily taken through the small entrance of a nesting-hole. These sticks presented a problem that Smoke had to solve for herself; they were longer than the width of the entrance to the petrol tin. The first one she brought was held in the middle and three unsuccessful attempts were made to force it through the hole, but she found it was too long and would not yield to pressure. She hopped to a perch in front of the tin and stared at the hole with an intent expression for a moment, then went back and deliberately stretched her head back – away from the hole – turned it to one

* In both these instances their expression, fidgety manners and strained poses showed they were really worried.

side so the stick was in length-wise position instead of across the entrance hole, and successfully got it through. It could not possibly have been chance, for the pose of stretching back and twisting her neck was most unnatural. It must have been a deliberate action, which appeared to be the result of her concentrated stare at the entrance hole. Every stick was then taken through in this same manner. Many such problems are continually confronting the nest-builder; they are solved by the individual intelligence of the bird. House-Martins have arrived at the same method of plastering their clay pellets as man uses in laying his bricks – overlapping the joins. Other species weave with the skill of basket makers and embroiderers, utilising with sense and artistry materials they can find and think fit. Intelligent application of their minds to nest-building is necessary to accomplish the work with so much perfection, variation in detail occurring although the pattern of the nest conforms to the species. And how is it the forefathers arrived at the wonderful patterns if not through using their intelligence?

Naturally, many actions in the daily round of a bird's life are automatic – so are many of ours. With birds or humans, actions become automatically performed through constant repetition. For instance:

1. A bird may take the same route to its nest, choosing exactly the same perches mechanically while mind and eyes are alert for enemies who may be watching their movements. When I am doing a garden job necessitating many journeys to the same spot, I find myself taking exactly the same route each time; by so doing the job is more quickly and easily performed. Birds likewise are helped by this routine, but if occasion makes it advisable they will alter their route although the habit of certain perches may have become very strongly formed. Sometimes no habit is formed, the bird always varying its route to the nest.

2. It may happen a bird continues to look for its nest in the accustomed place after someone has removed it a short distance away. Again there are similar traits in human behaviour, for if something is removed without our knowledge we may continue to search for it where we think it should be found and has always been kept although the thing in question may be easy to see in its altered position.

The above two points have been given as reasons for the automaton theory of bird behaviour. My experience of the latter has only shown that the bird becomes very distressed if her nest is moved a little way off, perhaps more because of the danger that interference might bring to the young than difficulty in seeing the nest a few feet away. Fear nearly always makes a parent bird afraid to go to its nest even if it has not been tampered with in this manner. Artificial tests for intelligence are generally misleading because of the complete alteration in a bird's behaviour under influence of fear.

Birds are also said to be lacking in intelligence because they seem not to recognise their own nestlings if they fall from the nest to the ground below it or are removed to another position nearby. But I have found they continue to feed their immature fledglings when they fly or fall from the nest too soon, or even if I place very immature young, fallen from a nest, into another improvised nest nearby. (See Chapter 1, a Robin incident. In this case it must be taken into consideration the bird has no fear of me so its actions are normal.)

If a naked nestling falls from the nest it is deserted by its parents. It would have no chance of survival in its exposed position, and it could not be brooded without neglect of those in the nest. If not consciously deserted it seems likely the completely naked, immature bird has not yet developed personality for recognition away from its surroundings. Instinct alone does not seem to account for birds' behaviour over deserting young. For instance, judgment often seems shown over giving the weakling a chance to recover, the parent distinguishing between accidental injury, causing temporary deformity and the incurable case. Fledglings in my garden have occasionally got their legs injured, but the parents continue to feed them during temporary deformity although they may seem hopelessly crippled. Often they recover after a day or two, but if good progress is not made the parent gives up feeding it. The Blackbird Oakleaf gave a good example of this. One of his newly-flown young broke its leg and seemed very ill for a day or two after the accident, but Oakleaf continued to feed it for a week in spite of its appearance being abnormal. At the end of the week it looked better, but the leg was permanently twisted; the bird was weakened and could never be strong. Oakleaf deserted it, despite cries for food, yet he was still feeding the rest of the brood. I took pity on the invalid and it was well fed for several weeks, but never became normally strong in the leg, and it was undersized and weakly. When driven from my garden in autumn it was incapable of fending for itself through the hardships of winter. Oakleaf had given the fledgling a chance to recover from the injury, and it seemed reasonable to think he acted with realisation of the facts. If he acted only on instinct why did he not desert the fledgling at once, when it seemed very ill and the foot was quite unusable?

I had another Blackbird who fed an undersized offspring much longer than those who were stronger and full-sized. I have seen other cases of this with many species, which shows that the parent does not necessarily desert the small fledgling who may never reach quite full stature.

Birds accidentally caught in a net or imprisoned in a room, etc., show panic when the human stranger approaches and they struggle more wildly to free themselves, making it harder to release them unharmed. But the person who has gained their confidence finds their behaviour intelligently responsive towards efforts to free them – not always easy if toes are entangled. Here is an incident that occurred recently. House-mice were doing much damage in my room, including an attack upon a new coat, strips being torn off the pockets to get at a nut inside. (My pockets generally contain bits of food for the birds.) In despair I set a mouse-trap in a corner, shielded by tin tray fortifications I thought no bird could move, although I intended to take away the trap at dawn. But I forgot. The following morning, while gardening near the window, I heard the terrible sound of a struggling creature in the trap – though it was supposed to kill instantaneously. Entering the room, I found a Great Tit had managed to pull aside a tin tray and had spotted the cheese on the trap, with the result he was caught round the neck. He had fluttered his wings and struggled desperately to free himself until I walked towards him repeating soothingly, 'It's all right, I'll let you free' – for birds understand the meaning of speech by its tone. Then he stopped struggling, and when I bent over him he looked up at me without any sign of fear or pain but an expectant expression in his eyes. Still talking softly to him, I pulled the trap and the bird very gently towards me, this being necessary before I could get both hands on the spring. He kept perfectly still and relaxed, his eyes on mine with that waiting expression. I expected he might struggle while I was lifting the spring, and this would make it difficult to free him without injury. But he had the intelligence to realise I was releasing him and kept quite still, his eyes calmly watching mine while I lifted the spring. He was freed unharmed. He gave a quick little shake to his ruffled feathers then flew out of the window with a subdued scold-note. Examining the trap to discover why he was not crushed, I found a small bend in the wire just where it closed over his neck; but for this he would have been killed outright. After a short preen outside, he returned to take food from my hand as usual, apparently none the worse for his experience. I am haunted by the sight of his lovely head pinned down on the trap, but grateful to have been spared causing a bird injury or death. The mice may do what they like, for I cannot set another trap in my rooms.

With birds continually flying round me, spying into everything I do, it is impossible to avoid catching their toes occasionally in shutting tins or drawers. Often Great Tits perch on the rim at the last moment before closing and I see them just in time to prevent serious damage, but sometimes their feet get a little hurt. They perch on me directly afterwards to examine their toes, passing their beaks down each toe, probably to moisten it with saliva. The accident never makes the bird fear me, he does not even fly out of the room for he realises it was not an intentional hurt. I have even gripped a Great Tit's head between my fingers once or twice when I was picking up something and the bird suddenly pounced at the same time. The Tit gave a short shriek but, directly I let go, with softly spoken apologies, he just gave a shake to his feathers and calmly looked up at me without the least suspicion of fear, although the sudden gripping of his head cannot have been comfortable and must have been a shock. Yet if I speak sharply to the bird – when no physical hurt has been suffered – he will be afraid and fly away from me until I change my tone of voice. How do birds come by such discrimination if not through using their intelligence?

Just as it is possible to assess from facial expressions and slight movements what a bird wants or is going to do, the bird can assess the human. I gave illustrations of this in Chapter 5 (bath preparations), and Chapter 1 (butter-dish tests), but here is another. If I hold out an unshelled nut to some of my Great Tits they look at it eagerly then up at my face with an expectant expression, watching for me to show signs of cracking it for them. I sometimes do this with a hammer, and directly I take up this tool certain intelligent ones fly to the window, waiting outside until the crack is over, when they immediately return with great eagerness of manner to receive the nut. They realise I am going to make a noise directly they see me with hammer and nut; the hammer alone or the nut alone never makes them fly to the window. Only certain Great Tits understand the sharp crack is going to happen, others hurriedly fly away when the noise is heard, except a few who are insensitive to the bang. The most intelligent and sensitive birds watch my face and actions, putting two and two together with astonishing speed in many such things as the above, even after once or twice seeing the action. Great Tits are especially full of curiosity at an early age, as seen in Chapter 2, Part 2 – Baldhead's curiosity over his parents' second brood. This may help to develop their powers of observation and intelligence. The same applies to some of the crow tribe, etc.

Birds understand the importance of watching eye expressions, not only among themselves but with the human. When my birds want me to throw food I am holding in my hand, they do not keep their eyes upon the food or the hand that throws it, but gaze searchingly into my eyes, this keen scrutiny being kept up until I either throw the food or move away. As well as fixing my eyes, they ask for the food to be thrown in ways that vary with the individual, but they never pay attention to the hand that holds the food; they are concerned only with how I am going to act, and their contact with the human is made through the eyes. In Chapter 1, I have already referred to their being able to interpret correctly my tone of voice or movements, in butter-dish experiments, etc. If they want to steal food, and I keep silent, they watch my eyes for signs of objection while going towards it and helping themselves. The birds who do not know me well behave in the same manner. If a piece of cheese or bread is on the floor near the window, a hungry stranger Blue Tit spies it and wonders if I shall object to his taking it. He cautiously enters, eyes fixed on mine while he takes the food then flies away. One Blue Tit coveted a large piece of bread-and-butter placed on the floor, which he was unable to lift, so by degrees he dragged it along with his feet, all the while fixing his eyes on the human's face until he got it outside and could eat without fear of disapproval. Blackbirds and other species generally behave in much the same manner.

This winter, for a week or two, I did some typing every day at a table beside my bed. The Great Tits have always before kept off the bed unless I am in it, although they hop over everything else in the room. But because I was busy so close to the bed two or three of them began hopping along it and perching there to eat food I gave them.

Directly I called 'Get off the bed' – the first time in rather a commanding tone – they obeyed and hopped either farther from me to their
favourite screen perch, or came closer to me, perching on my chair-
back or the table. After the first time, I repeated the words without a
commanding tone yet they understood, at once leaving the bed for
some other perch nearby. I then tried, in the same tone, saying other
words such as ' poke the fire,' but although they glanced up at me they
did not move from the bed. I tested them too often for it to have been
chance. Always they obeyed the words, 'Get off the bed,' or just, 'Off
the bed.' After three days they had reverted to their old habit of never
perching on it.

Birds have certain codes of behaviour which make their actions
appear to conform to a set pattern, but each bird has a personality of
its own and, if we study bird-law carefully and intimately, comparing
behaviour within the species, we find continual relaxations or elastic
variations of laws according to individual circumstances. (Chapter 3,
Part 1, Thief being allowed to bring his young into Blackie's territory;
Chapter 2, Part 1, Jane allowed into the Pugnacious Tits' territory
when she lost her mate, etc.) Sensible discrimination is shown over
many things in bird behaviour. These codes seem sometimes based
upon general recognition of the character of an individual, for I have
known a Blackbird, who was an exceptionally fine singer, keep order
in the garden as if he had some recognised influential position; whenever he saw two birds fighting – of any species – he stalked up to them
and immediately they stopped quarrelling. Having settled their dispute he flew back to his song perch and continued singing. Another
example, a Thrush, also a remarkably fine songster, who had such distinction or social superiority that even Blackbirds gave way before
him. Usually the Song-Thrush is chivvied by the Blackbird if both
come into close contact on the feeding-ground, but if something special in the way of food tempted this Thrush, he could walk calmly in
front of any Blackbird in my garden and they gave way before him. It
was an astonishing sight to see the Blackbirds allow this precedency. In
both cases it appeared to be the personality and perhaps special power
of song that gained this distinction, for neither were ever seen to fight
or display physical strength to gain superiority.

Bird behaviour is much dependent upon the character of the individual. Even finding and securing a mate is a varied process within the

species. It may be accomplished with very little display or preliminary courting or there may be much conspicuous wooing and ardent display, according to individuals and to circumstances. As will be mentioned in the following song chapters, there is infinite variation over quality and quantity of song within the species – as well, of course, as between the species – the same applying in the art of flight performances. All these individual differences must be taken into consideration when trying to get nearer an understanding of bird mind. The more familiar one becomes with each bird, the more noticeable it is that in all things birds have individuality. These differences may be great or they may seem to us very slight, but the fact that all this variation of intelligence, memory, emotions, etc., occurs within the species, affecting their behaviour, shows that although certain fundamental laws are obeyed instinctively, in the main, actions are not automatic, but controlled by the mind of the bird according to its character. To me, the grounds never seem secure for the definite statement continually made at the present time, that bird-mind is completely different from ours. Their sight and hearing has resemblances although some differences. (Birds give imitations that show they hear the sound as we hear it.) And if we compare reactions of birds to those of men, especially the human child, there are many points of resemblance, particularly where emotions are concerned. Bird-mind, within its limitations of intelligence, may have resemblances although naturally many differences. Development is, of course, on entirely different lines, but if there are not resemblances how is it that bird and man can arrive at as much understanding of each other when they become intimate?

Man has developed his brain at expense of the senses and lost some natural faculties or senses possessed by primitive tribes. Birds, in their wild, free life have these senses highly developed, particularly the sense of direction or homing sense, necessary because flight gives them power to travel vast distances away from their breeding grounds.

FLIGHT PERFORMANCES

Birds not only use flight as a natural means of locomotion, but in beautified forms as a means of expression, some species combining it with song. (See Chapter 12.) Many species spend hours of the day in the recreation of flight, as others spend hours in song. Flight is an art akin to music, with rhythm and feeling of movement as its foundation, a glorious means of expression that birds, with their emotional natures, know well how to use.

Some species, social in their habits, such as Waders, Starlings, etc., have developed flock-flight in unison to such perfection that the inquisitive human is for ever wondering how they achieve this simultaneous movement without a conductor to assist. Much has been written about this interesting subject. E. M. Nicholson in *How Birds Live* suggests that all birds in the flock are 'keyed up to a state of quickened responsiveness,' and 'like a dog waiting orders from a master' their minds are blank and alert to take leadership from any one bird in the flock who happens to turn. But the flocks vary from a very few birds to hundreds, and why should there always happen to be only one among them who turns, or perhaps two, the flock splitting? In my opinion, flight performances may be achieved in a manner comparable to musicians performing together. Musicians when playing are keyed up to a quickened responsiveness as birds are during these flights, and in good chamber music performances – without a conductor – the players feel together as one, not as separate individuals each playing a different part. They concentrate upon the music as a whole, not on their separate parts alone. All are swayed by the same impulse or inspiration, and each feels a supersensitive consciousness of the other player's interpretation, often to the point of feeling it slightly in advance. In playing, as in all actions, the mind must work in slight anticipation of action and this is particularly an important factor in quick passages. One might argue that it is the score from which musicians play that is their guide, but Zigeuner Bands play without written music, extemporising their different parts yet achieving the effect of a whole, all being inspired by the same wave of feeling. This also applies to Welsh part-singing, 'hwyl' is the Welsh term for this inspiration. Since musicians do not always play a composition exactly in the same manner, ensemble performances are ragged without this supersensitive anticipation. This might be described as intercommunication between individual minds under extraneous impulse.

As it is possible for humans of special sensibilities to combine together under the same emotional sway, it is likely that this would apply even more to birds, for they are admittedly quicker in emotional reaction. When under the excitement of performance, musicians are carried along by a living current that is a sort of life in itself, and they are not only thrilled themselves, but their audience can feel the thrill of their performances. When birds pass close to us, flying rhythmically in these simultaneous flights, the effect upon humans sensitive to such things is very strong; there is a thrill and excitement emanating from the flock; the birds' flight is felt as well as seen.

But when birds are flying to their feeding grounds or for other such practical purposes, there is not concentration upon flight as a performance and no tenseness of application to flight movement; they are not keyed up to emotional responsiveness and the result is not rhythmical as a whole. They then fly as if following one after another and no emotional thrill is felt emanating from the flock as they pass near the watcher.

There is much evidence that thought transference occurs among humans, this being generally accepted by scientists because of much existing proof. It is thought to be a natural faculty much neglected and decayed in modern man. There is reason for thinking birds possess this extra sense, intimate observation bringing cases that cannot be explained otherwise. (See Chapter 2, page 31.) Birds' senses play a large part in their lives; they have developed to a high degree sense of direction and of time; with the exception of smell, they have all the senses normally possessed by man in a well-developed form and there seems no reason to exclude the probability of their having this extra-sensory perception or telepathic communication in a simple form, by which many things in bird behaviour could be explained that are otherwise unaccountable.

Part Two

BIRD SONG

CHAPTER 9

Atmosphere and Song

It was a bleak December day and no birds were on the wing in the valley of the Sussex Ouse. Dejected-looking groups of Daws and Rooks were straddled upon the fences, and many Gulls sat hunched along the riverside. All looked too depressed for flight or food and not one bird-note was to be heard. The still air was damp and shuddery, a grim sulkiness seemed settled upon everything. The grey downs looked toneless and dead, fields and marshes were drab and cheerless, and the river flowing between them was lifeless, dark-coloured and oily.

Slowly the grey sky darkened with gathering clouds and by the time a distant bend in the river was reached it seemed night would fall at noon. Firle Beacon and Mount Caburn were like shadows of themselves, while towards the sea and westwards the downs were blurred and indistinguishable from the blackness of overhanging clouds. There was an eerie quiet that did not belong to day.

Then suddenly a Thrush broke the heavy winter silence by a full, rich song and at the same moment a small shaft of sunlight fell on the smooth peak of Mount Caburn so that its shadowed form was crowned with gold, which slowly spread until this shapely hill stood all alight while everything around as yet remained in gloom.

The Thrush, in his tree near the river, sang as if spring had come, while the sun stretched long silvery feelers from under the great cloud-bank that was gradually drifting apart, and through a widening rift the sun's face was slowly revealed. Firle Beacon was touched with sunlight which crept along that whole range, then into the Ouse valley, turning fields from drabness to glowing green. The grazing cattle, before unseen in the gloom, stood out in rich colours against the grass, and the river, now rippled by a faint breeze, sparkled and became alive.

Two horses, lying in a field across the water, stood up, stretched themselves and swished their tails as if expectant of summer flies. And, indeed, it seemed that the sun, blazing through the rift in those sombre clouds, had an intensified brilliance unknown to mid-winter.

Now all birds found their voices and wings. Cries of Peewits came from over the marsh and a flock wheeled high in the air; many Field-fares called as they passed overhead, flying to the trees where the Thrush still sang; the forlorn-looking Rooks roused themselves and took to the wing, cawing eerily as if shaking off evil dreams; the crouching Gulls arose all together and as they sailed and circled above, it seemed they expressed by flight what the Thrush was saying by song.

A Great Black-backed Gull was there, majestic in movement, slow and powerful in his measured turns, as if he timed his flight of slow planing in small circles for some momentous purpose ordained by the world above. A small bush-covered headland jutted out close to the river and over this he curved his flight, always rounding with slow precision, his great wings and tail full-spread.

Thick clouds soon covered the sun again. Elation passed, but the effect of that rift was still felt all around. Eagerness replaced gloom. Two Snipe flew swiftly across the marsh, all birds sought their feeding grounds and now not one Gull or Rook remained crouching forlornly alongside the river.

Perhaps the most wonderful thing about birds is their song. The more one listens to their music, gathering knowledge and understanding of their musical language, the more beauty the subject holds. Song is an emotional outlet, a bird's heart goes into his music, so by full and intimate appreciation of his song we get nearer understanding a bird's nature.

Being highly strung and easily roused, many different kinds of emotions will make them break into song. They are very sensitive to atmosphere. Especially the transitional lights between day and night rouse a bird to his fullest expression by song. When the stars are fading the dawn-chorus begins. Lark, Blackbird or another the first to sing – for dawn-song has no set rules – and while the earth gathers light more and more birds fill the air with stirring song, giving their fullest to the awakening day. At sundown their song has a quieter tone, in keeping with nature's mood of peace and beauty as evening falls.

Sudden and unexpected changes of atmosphere, such as sunlight after storm, also bring response from birds even in mid-winter, as shown in the above episode. That song in the sunlight on December 21st was the only bird-music heard until the turn of the year, a long spell of exceptionally bleak and gloomy weather having lasted for most of that month.

Birds love the sunlight. Towards sundown in my garden many will perch where they can face the sinking sun, as the shadows spread to them they shift their positions, perhaps a few twigs higher catch the sun's rays for a short while. But the shadows creep after them so they move again, the trees keeping the last rays of sunlight being full of birds preening or just watching the sun going down. For a while they are very quiet, not one bird will feed or sing during these moments of hush that precede sundown. When the sun has sunk very low on the horizon the atmosphere changes and birds are stirred to music while the skies grow brilliant and earth slowly darkens, the last notes of Thrush and Blackbird falling with heightened beauty on the gathering dusk.

In spring it may happen that bird-song is silenced when, for some days, an easterly wind clings like a blight over the land. The Blackbird, an especially sensitive singer, is often the first to go silent. Although, by the calendar, the time is ripe for him to unfold the great talent he hides under dark feathers for so much of the year, precious days of his fulfilment are lost. The east wind seems not to have affected the organs of his voice, for his chuckle and call-notes are loud and clear. His mate may continue nesting and brooding her eggs, which is her creative work, but his creative spark is put out by the chill of the atmosphere. When not parading his territory, stalking the neighbour Blackbirds, he spends much time perched motionless and quiet on a tree. At the first sign of change in the weather, often sensed by birds many hours before the human, the Blackbird and all other songsters take to music again in full measure, while the kindlier wind brings softening of atmosphere and the sky is swept clear of the east-wind blight.

The quality of bird-song is also affected by their surrounding atmosphere. Birds bred and remaining in the confinement of large towns have less spirit and variety in their songs than those who have the freedom of the countryside and choose leafy gardens or wild woodlands for their homes. Partly, this is because they are influenced by the sounds they hear around them. A thrush may sing better for having heard a Nightingale, and the Robin whose home has been where Warblers' sing sometimes blends a little of the beauty of their songs into the phrases of his own. I think this applies to many species, for musicians learn from one another and birds have ears alert for every sound. But besides this imitative influence over their phrases, the actual atmosphere of scene seems to affect the quality of song. My earliest impression of the Willow-Warbler was that he sang best in quiet places where many flowers grew. (He is not, of course, a roadside bird like the Whitethroats, some Finches and Buntings.) I have noticed since that he appears sensitive to surroundings, and it seems his song varies emotionally according to Nature's mood. Although his music is usually gently reflective, I once heard him entirely change the character of his song.

It was in April, but a heavy snowstorm had covered the South Downs. Sunshine had thawed the snow in a sheltered hollow under Ditchling Beacon, but the blossoming blackthorn, which filled the hollow, rivalled the dazzling whiteness of the snow-clad hill above. The only sound, ringing through the stillness, was the voice of a Willow-Warbler, incessantly shouting a triumphant song as he flew backwards and forwards with unusually buoyant flight over the tops of those snow-white bushes. His loud, exultant tones were not characteristic, but the shape of the song and purity of voice remained unchanged. It seemed the brilliance of the scene with the first blossoming of spring had made him shout his song of exaltation while making joyous flights over the flowering bushes. If it was merely that the thaw had freed his lungs, why should he always choose that aerial pathway across the blossom for his song?

A few days later I returned to the same hollow. The snow had melted from the downs, the blossom faded from the bushes, and the soft greens of downland turf and unfolding leaves replaced the dazzling brilliance of the former scene. Among the same bushes the Willow-Warbler was singing, but this time there was no buoyant flight above them and the spirit of love and tenderness shone through his mellow notes. A gentleness, born of the maturer spring, was in his voice as in the scene.

All these things show a high degree of emotional receptivity and responsiveness – perhaps best appreciated by the artistically susceptible mind. In bird-song there is evidence of so much that is beyond the limits of automatism, and those who have not the sensitive ear or opportunity to acquire really intimate knowledge and understanding of bird-song are much hampered in their power to estimate a bird's nature. The fact that musical talent varies individually – within species – as much as among human performers of music is not compatible with the theory of minds that only work automatically, without individual intelligence. This variation of talent is not only a question of voice quality, but such things as the material of the song or musical composition; the interpretation of the composition, especially with Blackbirds; and the technical ability, for there are some who have to work much longer than others to acquire song-technique, various degrees of proficiency being finally achieved. Also, the way birds work shows much musical intelligence.

Illustrations of all these points will be given in the analysis of bird-song that follows. These analytical chapters, beginning with technique of bird-music approached from a new angle, may perhaps help some readers to explore for themselves the vast field of interest that lies behind listening to bird-song. The following chapter is entirely technical and analytical, but can easily be skipped by those not specially interested in this subject.

CHAPTER 10

Analysis of Technique in Bird Song

Analysis of technique in bird-song is helpful for learning to follow the rapid intricacies of many songs so that individuals within the species can be distinguished by subtle differences in their song. Recognising the individual Blackbird or Thrush by his particular tunes or phrases is not difficult, provided the listener has a good ear and is alert for imitations within the species – for a good singer, especially among Blackbirds, often has his best ideas cribbed by neighbours. (See Imitation, page 153.) But the song of many species is of such fine texture and the pace so quick that the human ear if untrained, has difficulty over following the song in detail, many listeners even being unable to distinguish between different species whose music has some slight resemblance, as for instance, the Blackcap and Garden-Warbler. But the more familiar one becomes with these rapid and complicated songs, the more apparent are the individual differences.

The birds themselves would not have our difficulty in recognising individuals by their song. They are more sensitive to sound and degrees of sound within their range. As already mentioned in a previous chapter, time to them is slower than to us, their pulse faster, their temperature higher and their emotional reactions quicker. So, to them, the pace of their fastest musical phrases would be easy to follow and their sharper hearing would make the subtle inflections of voice easy to distinguish. But we need to learn these subtleties of their musical language.

Realisation of the following technical points is, I think, helpful for better understanding of bird-music.

1. Birds use a musical scale containing more intervals within the octave than our scale, which is adjusted by temperament to twelve notes – the chromatic scale of semitones.* Our ears are accustomed to

---

* Definition: 'Our scale is modified by a system of compromise whereby the tones, generated with the vibrations of a ground tone, are mutually modified and

this scale, with a semitone as the smallest interval, but birds use freely many notes in between the semitone, even smaller than the demi-semitone, as can be most easily noticed when they sing a rapid phrase of many notes descending down the scale, yet the passage has only fallen one or two tones, according to our musical notation. These intervals, smaller than semitones, I term intertones. Birds, therefore, have an infinite variety of notes, each with its harmonics or secondary notes which accompany any single note, their scale, in fact, being the natural unlimited scale of Nature. Larks and Warblers employ to perfection numbers of intertones; they sound natural to our ears although impossible to transcribe accurately, for our scale and musical language is different.

2. Timbre is one of the most important factors in recognition of the songs of different species, but birds make continual alterations in the sound of their notes without alteration of the timbre (apart from change of interval), just as a human singer alters his words yet keeps the same quality of timbre or voice. As we cannot say that birds use different words or vowels, this alteration is, I think, best described by the word phone.* For instance, when the Chiffchaff sings, the chiff is a different phone from chaff, although the timbre is unaltered; similarly, the Cuckoo uses two phones, but many species employ a great number of different phones which give colour and variety to their music. Transcribing phones into such sounds as 'pee, tee, tew,' etc., never seems satisfactory because people appear to hear these phones differently, 'tee' to one person being more like 'chew' to another, and so on. But whatever the phones sound like to each person, if these are consciously noticed and the phone changes memorised, it assists the mind to take in the details of bird-song, this making rapid passages easier to follow and identification of individuals within the species then become possible, even with the most complicated songs.

3. Birds, like human musicians, make much use of accelerando, ritardando and tempo rubato. The musical term, *rubato*, means an elastic treatment of the notes without disturbing the rhythm, some notes being accelerated and others retarded so that the balance is kept and

---

in part cancelled, until their number is reduced to the actual practical scale of twelve tones.'

* Definition: 'Voice sound as vowel or consonant.'

the rhythm as a whole unaffected. It will often be noticed in listening to bird-song that a sudden or gradual accelerando – or hastening – of quick notes is followed by dwelling on long notes or one long note elaborated by a trill. For example, the Wood-Warbler, with perfect artistry, makes a very effective use of a gradual accelerando that leads to a sustained note with an exquisite trill.

I find that listening to bird-song occasionally with an analytical mind helps appreciation of the perfection of their music without detracting from the emotional pleasure.

In the following pages much use will be made of the words inter-tone, phone and rubato, so it should be remembered that

> *intertones* mean intervals within the semitone;
>
> *phone* means type of sound that alters within the timbre;
>
> *rubato* means elastic give and take of note values within the rhythm.*

4. Rhythm is the foundation of bird-song as of all music. The character and emotion of the music depends to a great extent upon the rhythm. Each species of bird seems to be born with a rhythm of its own – which shows even in the fledgling cries – as with human races there is characteristic rhythm in their native music.

For purposes of technical analysis the following classification into types of rhythm is, I think, helpful, but the unavoidable imperfections of such groupings must be taken into account. Naturally, there is overlapping of types and no exact line can be drawn between them.

TYPES OF RHYTHM AND TECHNICAL ANALYSIS OF SPECIES

TYPE I. – CUCKOO (male); CHIFFCHAFF; DOVES, etc. Birds who have only one song in a set rhythm of the simplest possible form.

They hardly achieve rhythm in its bigger sense; it might be described as expressing a few notes rhythmically. Their song depends much upon phone; for example, 'cuck-cuck' would be feeble but 'cuc-koo'

---

* Rhythm definitions:
  'The united sum of different parts into a unit.'
  'An expression of the instinct for order in sound.'

is a masterpiece considering its simplicity. Timbre, phone and delivery make the character of these songs even more than the simple rhythm, for the phrases 'cuc-koo' and 'chiffchaff' are rhythmically of the same balance yet totally different in effect. There are many people who mistake a Great Tit's 'tee-chū'* song for the Chiffchaff's, which is really not alike. Both birds use two notes and two phones, but these have not any resemblance, and the timbre of these species is very different, as is the style of their delivery. The Chiffchaff sounds controlled and quietly precise, the Great Tit recklessly bold, as if flinging his all into every note. The Great Tit should not even be included in this type, often four notes or more are used, making the 'tee-chū' song very variable in rhythm, and it depends upon the individual bird what tune is sung. Also, this Tit has many other songs and conversational pieces. (See page 164.) Some Chiffchaffs have original ways of grouping their two-noted phrase in its repetition, this making recognition of the individual possible.

It is often possible to distinguish individual Cuckoos by consistent choice of certain intervals, pitches, and slight variations of the two phones. The Dove species have monotonous songs and, I think, their dreamy crooning does not vary enough with the individual for recognition to be possible by song, although I have heard Turtle-Doves whose notes had some distinctive peculiarities. Besides the 'turr-tle-dove' song from which the name is derived, this species croons on one upturned note evenly repeated, and also one note upturned followed by two downturned notes, all evenly repeated.

TYPE 2. — CHAFFINCH; YELLOWHAMMER; WREN; DUNNOCK; CORN-BUNTING, etc. Birds whose song conforms to a set but much more elaborate rhythm.

The rhythm of these songs is outstanding, the balance of long and short notes being musically perfect. (Without balance there is no 'order in sound,' and good rhythm depends upon perfection of balance.) Owing to the speed of these songs phone plays a less important part than in Type 1, except in the finale of Chaffinch and Yellowhammer. Song abbreviations and shortened variants are heard especially in

* Handbook term.

early spring and late summer, but during the height of the season each bird usually repeats his full song without varying the set rhythmic pattern. Individuals in these species are often distinguishable for they do not all sing quite alike in detail. Chaffinches are distinguishable by distinct differences of intervals in the trills as well as the cadence (or finale). But each bird repeats his own version in full song. Some Chaffinches sing their trills descending in approximate thirds, and finish with extra brilliance, others keep to closer intervals, and a few seem unable to achieve the customary flourish at the cadence, the song being rounded off lamely or clumsily. Their delivery is always boldly rhythmical. As with the Chaffinch, the Yellowhammer's song at its fullest has a cadence of very definite changes in intervals and phones. Their songs bear no resemblance, but in both cases the cadence is the feature of the song, although some singers in each species seem incapable of performing both of the final notes. The Yellowhammer, in the fullest edition of his song, finishes with two notes that form a rallentando, dreamy in effect. Although the individual varies the detail and interpretation of the song at times, it is always kept within the same set rhythmic pattern. Both Yellowhammer and Corn-Bunting sing in an easy, effortless style suitable to the heat of summer afternoons when they alone keep up continuous song.

The Wren's delivery is so bold for such a small bird that it is sometimes startling if heard very close. The strong rhythm of the full song is set to pattern without much individual difference even in detail. They sing many abbreviated variants. The Dunnock's (Hedge Sparrow's) rhythm is rather sing-song in effect, and he sings in a neat, precise manner, a little as if repeating something learnt by heart. Both species are hard to distinguish individually by their songs.

TYPE 3. — REED-WARBLER; SEDGE-WARBLER; BLACKCAP; GARDEN-WARBLER; WILLOW-WARBLER ; LARK; LINNET; GOLDFINCH, etc. Birds whose rhythms are free and varied, the accented beat changing — especially in subsong. The delivery of these elaborated rhythms is also complicated by the use of tempo rubato.

The Reed-Warbler's song is a good example. He sometimes works up an accelerando of quick notes to a great speed then balances the whole by proportionately retarded slower notes. He often changes the accent, thus making cross-rhythms. Here is an example of one

Reed-Warbler's rhythm, to show changing accents. This was rapidly taken down while he sang. The accented beats are correct as far as it is possible to notate, but there were, of course, many notes between these crotchets. The bird-scale intertones make any transcription of the notes in their song impossible except for rhythmic outline.

The delivery is intensely rhythmic and full of energy, the outstanding feature being rhythm, but the more familiar one becomes with individual singers the more conscious one is of phone changes, which heighten the colour effect of the song. Many of the phrases contained in his song are imitative, but he weaves them with continuity into an original composition with rhythm that is entirely his own.

The Sedge-Warbler is very much more imitative and he uses much irregular rubato which is not always well balanced – but this is often exaggerated by nervousness of the listener. He has not such a strong and decisive rhythm of his own as the Reed-Warbler.

The Blackcap and Garden-Warbler also create in free and varied rhythms, sometimes with use of rubato. The Garden-Warbler uses more trills but has less variety of interval and rhythm than the Blackcap, whose timbre is purer and rings more clearly, the notes usually lengthening towards the cadence with a crescendo. Individual Blackcaps are much easier to distinguish than Garden-Warblers because their song is more melodic.

It may be thought by many that the Willow-Warbler repeats one phrase in a set rhythmic pattern as do birds in Type 2. His song is of such delicate texture that only the experienced listener will realise this is not the case. His song of varying, falling intertones on a diminuendo seems to be sung with one phone of many inflections that gradually lead into the phone being changed at the cadence – on the last two notes. Much rubato is used, the song beginning slowly and accelerating as the tone diminishes.

Distinguishing all these Warblers within the species is possible by noticing their individual rhythmic patterns, phones, cadences and other details.

Sky-Larks and Tree-Pipits have great freedom of rhythm, the former, of course, having many more tunes woven into their song. The Tree-Pipit gives a wonderful example of ritardando as he glides down to a tree-top singing 'seea-seea-seea.'* There is much individual variation in the material of the Lark's song. The Tree-Pipit varies more in the way he sings and individual birds make curtailments of the full song, many phrases then never being sung (see page 177).

Both Linnet and Goldfinch use rubato and crescendos in their songs. The Goldfinch's gay and spontaneous-sounding song with its sparkling rhythms is more brilliant than the Linnet's gentler and more subtle music. The delivery is fluent and light, a Linnet's more serious.

The Greenfinch's heavier, monotonous song seems to verge between Type 2 and Type 3, for it is not quite set in rhythm nor is there much freedom or change. But he has a way of singing his song in fragments; when he gives it in full it has some variation although he is not a good example of Type 3 rhythm.

TYPE 4. – BLACKBIRD; THRUSH; ROBIN; NIGHTINGALE, etc. Birds whose song consists of many distinctly different phrases in different rhythms, sung with a moment's pause between each phrase. In their subsongs the separate phrases are all woven together into one continuous stream of song, often lasting several minutes and sung very quietly.

Blackbirds are composers of many phrases or tunes of entirely different rhythms, sung with slight pauses separating the tunes. Each bird composes his own melodies, although much cribbing goes on especially among the less gifted singers (see page 154 on cribbing). Their song is much more akin to human music than that of any other species, some of their tunes being in approximately correct classical notation of interval and time signature (using compound and simple time). Each bird appears to try for variety of effect by singing his tunes at different paces, adding embellishments, altering the key, singing in major and minor modes, using staccato and legato.† The Blackbird even tries turning his phrase upside down. All these ways of treating a

---

* Handbook term.
† Staccato definition: sharply detached – legato; smoothly slurred.

tune are in the human composer's technique. He varies phones and has a wide range of intervals in his songs. His delivery is calm and controlled. Vibrato* is used effectively and with great discrimination. Blackbirds are very easy to recognise individually by their song because of its more human technique and the difference in each bird's tunes.

The Song-Thrush also composes many phrases of different rhythms, but they are shorter than the Blackbird's and sung twice or three times consecutively before he makes a half-second pause then begins his next phrase. This repetition gives rhythmical balance to the song as a whole; without it the effect would be choppy because of the shortness of each phrase and the different rhythmical beats between one phrase and another. The song depends much upon delivery, which is always boldly rhythmic. Some phrases in the song are common to many within the species, but each bird composes original ones as well and even those not invented by the singer have individual touches so that recognition by song is very easy. The Thrush sings with little variation of tone level – crescendo or rubato, etc., being hardly consistent with the shortness of each phrase.

Both Blackbird and Thrush have quiet subsongs, consisting of the material used in full song, but strung together without any break, excepting some connecting notes which are dwelt on. These linking notes are call-notes, chuckle-notes and occasionally an imitative phrase from another bird is included. All is sung very quickly and quietly, concentrated listening being necessary to pick out the details for analysis.

The Mistle-Thrush is a much less enterprising composer than Blackbird or Song-Thrush, but his type of song and quality of voice more resembles the former species. The rhythms of his song are comparatively simple, the range of intervals usually smaller and there is less change of phone and length value of notes, compared to the Blackbird. Individuals can be distinguished by their tunes, but recognition is not as easy in many cases as with Blackbirds, for although each bird makes his own tunes there is similarity between them very often and also much imitation within the species.

---

* Vibrato is often incorrectly termed as tremolo and perhaps better understood by this misnomer.

The Robin has much variety of rhythm and phone. The type of rhythm in his song as a whole is Warbler-like, but the form is different and corresponds with the Thrush tribe. His delivery and rubato vary according to his state of mind when singing, for he uses song more than any other species for a variety of territorial purposes, singing during autumn and winter as well as in nesting season. In calm moods his cadenza-like passages of chromatic intertones are often accelerated, followed by dwelling on long notes at the cadences, the rubato being well balanced. But in autumn disputes for territory his rubato runs riot and his delivery sometimes becomes strident and forced, he uses marked inflections of voice, accentuating certain notes in some phrases so that they convey totally different effects than when sung at ease after the dispute. Much of his song is common to the species, but some Robins have original ideas.

His subsong has great fluency of rhythm and contains a number of imitations from other species' songs and call-notes, as well as a miniature representation of all his own phrases, often linked together with two or three sighing notes, the first slightly accented, but all in the same whispered tones as the rest of the subsong.

Like the Thrush, the Nightingale depends much upon delivery and technique for the effects of his song. He sings many phrases in different rhythms – a slight pause between each – these being common to the species, although there are variants of the set phrases. Outstanding features of his song are the uses he makes of crescendos, phones and trill technique. Owing to the set pattern of each phrase, individuals cannot so easily be distinguished as in the case of Blackbirds and Thrushes, who compose their phrases individually. Occasionally a Nightingale may be heard to give an imitative phrase.

As with all songsters, there is much variation in ability, some Nightingales singing much more beautifully than others, so that recognition of the bird individually is by his way of singing the phrases, more than by the music he sings.

The Wood-Warbler and Tree-Creeper are both overlaps between types, for they sing two set songs, each in a different rhythm, and these two songs are sung at different times, quite separately. The Wood-Warbler's second song is not performed as often as the trill song previously mentioned on page 138. It consists of one note – the phone 'tway' – repeated with a big crescendo-ritardando, a perfect contrast to the trill song, which works up an accelerando on one note. It is remarkable that the timbre of these two songs is quite different, the trill song being high-pitched and a little thin-sounding, the 'tway' song mellow and exceptionally full-voiced.

The Tree-Creeper has one song which he sings fairly frequently and it may be heard all the year round. The rhythm is very definite and he sings it with much emphasis, making it sound like a miniature bugle-call. The other song is only sung during mating season – at least, I have only heard it at this time – and the tone is soft and secretive-sounding. It is a rhythmical grouping of notes that resemble their main call-note. Unlike the other song, there is no change of phone, but some slight variations of interval occur. The few notes of which the song consists are usually sung on an accelerando.

The Redstart and Pied Flycatcher overlap between Type 2 and Type 3. Both commence their song in a set pattern and rhythm, but finish in free style with much variation – often imitative, but I should mention that I have only heard one Pied Flycatcher, so am not able to judge if this is usual to his species. The following pages, analysing the songs of many species separately, will include a variety of things I have noticed about these songsters.

CHAPTER 11

Songs of Warblers and Thrush Tribes

CHIFFCHAFF

Bird-song, like all music, impresses according to the receptive ability and mood of the listener. Associations often influence our feelings towards the song of a species. For me the Chiffchaff's song is coloured with remembrances of childish visions. I first heard it from bed one early morning when very young and the mysterious tip-tap puzzled me much until I decided it came from a fairy blacksmith, hammering on a miniature anvil, making tiny horseshoes for fairy steeds. Listening to the song brought much delight to me and I continued to picture the fairy workman until some weeks later I heard an older member of the household say rather peevishly, 'I suppose that monotonous sound must come from some bird or other. It's been going on all day and gets on my nerves.' What a difference between the two impressions! It seems general for the Chiffchaff's song to be welcomed chiefly because this is the first migrant voice we hear in the woods and the sound is so essentially associated with early spring. But to me, there is still an air of mystery about this bird's song, some fairylike charm in his voice and in the restraint of his rhythmic beats, suggestive of secrets that belong to the woods.

A few individuals break away from the set song of the species. I have heard a young bird in autumn venture upon a few imitative phrases and call-notes of other species, which he inserted between 'chiff-chaffs.' The following spring the same original song came from a copse a quarter of a mile distant from where the young bird had sung the previous autumn. It was probably the same bird. The Chiffchaff, like many other species, includes the baby-cry in his song during a certain period of the nesting season.

WILLOW-WARBLER

The Willow-Warbler's song has, I think, the most intimate appeal of all the species. It goes straight from heart to heart, where there is true sympathy between bird and man. Each note seems to be delivered with loving care, especially after nesting begins. The rapidity of utterance and strength of tone sound thoughtfully graduated as the pure, sweet notes gently fall, then rising a little, fall again to a softer cadence. Often two or three repetitions of this diminuendo phrase are linked as if sung in one long breath, the tide of song smoothly ebbing and flowing, and sometimes sinking to the softest murmur. The purity of tone and exquisite simplicity of utterance make it the most perfect bird-music.

It is interesting to hear the young bird gradually shaping his song. The Willow-Warbler's fledgling cry is a wispy note like a gentle sigh. When he leaves the nest he repeats it continually but without sound of urgency, already showing the characteristic gentleness of the adult's rhythm. As the fledgling grows the cry strengthens very gradually, the Willow-Warbler's voice always being fairly soft. Usually in June the young bird begins to shape this note into a halting phrase of five or six notes, roughly outlining the future song. These notes have not yet purity or sweetness, nor is there control of tone value or free use of gracefully falling intertones. But the youngster seems practising towards this end. One or two notes are sung proportionately too loud, making the phrase sound jerky. He tries again and again, giving slow emphasis to each note as if to gain control of tone value. Gradually the slow emphasis turns into a caressing note and the husk of song has more of the adult's appealing sweetness. The youngster sings fitfully, but soon the caressing notes flow freely, the phrase is now expanded and the husk filled in with gently-flowing intertones that fall on a diminuendo, the line beautifully softened by varying little upward curves. The full beauty of expression and tone is not heard until the bird returns the following spring.

Then the Willow-Warbler sheds his lovely song all day among the fresh spring greenery, and when his mate starts to brood her eggs a careful listener can often hear the wispy baby-cry that seemed

forgotten long ago, reappearing attached to the beginning of the perfected song, now sung more gently, but more beautifully than ever.

BLACKBIRD

As well as possessing the most lovely mellow voice, the Blackbird has
imaginative genius. The moods of his tunes are very diverse, most
often beautiful, calm and reposeful, sometimes drolly humorous or
weird in effect, and often they are pastoral in character (these being
usually in six-eight time). Each bird's song is compiled of many such
tunes, composed by himself then sung with improvised variations of
the original idea if he thinks fit. Sometimes he leaves the tune unaltered
when he has it perfected.

One Blackbird actually composed the opening phrase of the Rondo
in Beethoven's violin concerto. (This was not imitation; I can vouch
for his not having heard the concerto played.) At first he sang:

Then a few days later the last note was altered and he sang the complete phrase twice, exactly as in the beginning of Beethoven's Rondo,
only of course higher pitched.

For the rest of the season this tune often figured among others in his
song. Sometimes he sang the phrase only once and he occasionally
reverted to his first idea, making a pause on the long-held last note, to
which he added an effective vibrato.

His interpretation of the Rondo varied. If the tune was sung only once he took it slowly, with smooth phrasing; when sung with the repeat, the pace was quickened towards the end each time of singing the phrase, a rubato effect that added brilliance to the performance — when sung by a Blackbird.

Perhaps it is fair to mention that in the score of Beethoven's Rondo the first crotchet — the note marked *slow* — always has *Tenuto* written above it, an indication that the note must be held, this being what the Blackbird did with exaggeration at times.

Blackbirds' tunes often do not come to them complete the first time of singing. It is interesting listening to touches being added which make the half-formed idea musically complete. Here is another example. This tune was first sung:

After a few days the Blackbird introduced a chromatic semitone which formed an effective triplet in the last half of the first bar:

This alteration made an incomparable amount of difference; the effect was graceful and charming, and it was sung with excellent musical interpretation, from a human standpoint. The downward slurred octave in the second bar was sung glidingly, giving a caressing touch that was in keeping with the chromatic triplet. He sang this for several days, then came a test of his musical judgment — to a human musician extremely interesting to witness. He tried the effect of altering the triplet into four semiquavers, making the tune:

He sang this a few times, but discarded it, returning to the triplet which he stuck to for the rest of the season and following years. He was absolutely right, for the last alteration was an overload which completely spoilt the feeling of the tune, whereas the triplet had made it perfect. This bird, called Fields, was full of original ideas and some of them were weird, humorous and mysterious, through the introduction of low-toned staccato notes and other technical experiments not usual in a Blackbird's song, but the good composers seem to try everything within range of their voice.

Listening to the Blackbird composing, it seems some intellectual understanding guides his musical gifts. He has certainly advanced along lines of classical human music far more than any other bird. As with most species there is much individual difference in ability. One Blackbird sang a Bach phrase, which may have been copied from hearing me play Bach on the violin. There was a short trill on one note which he had some difficulty in singing neatly at first, but after much practice he got it slick and clear. Then he began experiments of embellishing Bach's music by doubling the length of the trill and adding a similar trill to another note in the phrase. He was an exceptionally fine singer and the result was very lovely – flute-like in effect. He included this elaborated tune in his repertoire for three years. The second year a neighbour Blackbird, Thief, tried to crib it, but the trills were beyond his vocal technique. After a squeaky struggle he abandoned the attempt. (Thief's fondness for stealing tunes was mentioned in his biography.)

The Blackbird's trick of ending some of his phrases with high squeaky notes reminds me of certain human composers who formed a habit of declaring the finality of a movement by some untoward flourish, often high harmonics in violin compositions. But the finest

Blackbird singers usually end their melodies suitably (without use of artificial harmonics!).

The adult Blackbird's warbled subsong has a deeper, more tenor sound than any other bird's subsong and the smoother melodies he weaves into this music stand out clearly, with legato effect, among the embroidery of 'chuckle-notes,' 'chooks' and other notes which bind together his tunes into one long, continuous song. These 'chuckle-notes' are rather clumsily conspicuous at times in the subsong, for they are higher pitched than the rest of this music. (Thrush and Robin include chuckles that are imitative into their smoothly-flowing sub-songs without these being noticeable — for their subsongs are higher pitched and taken at a faster speed.)

Youngster Blackbirds have little melody in this soft music when first they begin to croon to themselves. They sometimes listen to adults and soon their subsong contains one or two tunes that later are voiced aloud. The following incident is an example of a listening youngster — written on the spot, while watching the birds.

September 25th, 1948; 5 p.m. An adult Blackbird, Fields, is perched high on a tree-branch, facing the evening sun, warbling a continuous and beautiful subsong, many full-song phrases interwoven between other notes. A young male flies to the same tree, perches within three yards of Fields and gazes at him with a listening expression. Fields stops singing and turns his back to the youngster. All is quiet for a few minutes. The youngster shows impatience. He turns round on his perch, keeps looking at Fields and opening and shutting his beak. (Birds often do this when wanting to be given food or other things. In this case, as subsequent behaviour showed, he wanted song.) Presently Fields begins singing his quiet song again. The youngster edges closer and, facing the same direction, fluffs out his feathers in exact imitation of Fields' pose. Again he has the listening expression; I feel sure he is taking a lesson from the older bird's singing. Always any slight alteration in Fields' pose is copied by this youngster. The song continues for half an hour, both birds remaining almost without movement, except that the black-robed tutor sometimes turns his head slightly while still singing and his eyes rest on the listening youngster, whose gaze is always upon the master musician. There is an air of deep content and absorption on the faces of both birds. The youngster's newly-grown black attire has less depth of tone than the older bird's richness of hue and the young Blackbird's beak is dark while Fields' is golden in colour. At last Fields stops singing, stretches himself and hops to the very end of the bough; the youngster copies this stretch exactly, in every detail of movement then hops slowly after him. Fields calls loudly, 'Shreeeee!' and flies off, the youngster at his heels. 'Shreeeee' is a note used on certain occasions, when wishing to be conspicuous, etc. (See page 156.)

I have heard an unusual song, of an entirely different type, come from a Blackbird. It alarmed me on first hearing for it sounded like a hysterical Song-Thrush going mad through some kind of torture and hoarsely shouting a jumbled medley of song in reaction to fright. Hurrying to the bird with ideas of saving it from disaster, I discovered it was the passionate love-song of a Blackbird in the last throes of wooing a provocative female, who led him a chase, round and round in small circles, on the roof of my wood-shed. He was getting more and more excited as the chase grew faster; his neck was stretched out, head-feathers were ruffled, eyes glittering and beak opened to let fling this volley of explosive-sounding song. She often threw glances over her shoulder in return, while leading him this last dance, the culmination of many weeks slow stalking chases up and down the lawn. Suddenly she flew to a branch beside the shed and mating took place.

The curious thing about this song was that it consisted of many short notes and phrases typical of a Song-Thrush, not Blackbird. There was no repetition, as in the Thrush's song and not a moment's pause; the voice and delivery were uncharacteristic. The whole performance was like an operatic scene with the performers over-dramatising their parts, the roof-top in its setting of tree branches making perfect stage scenery. The few times I have heard this dramatic love-song it has always been directly prior to mating, but it does not appear of common occurrence. This Blackbird did not commence his ordinary song until a week later. Usually I find Blackbirds have mated before giving time to full song. Contrary to the theory that one purpose of song is to attract females to the territory of males 'in a position to breed and ready to receive mates,' the female comes to the male often many weeks before he commences song, this applying to many species. (The Chaffinch uses call-notes for communication when his mate is first seen on his. territory – but I notice the female appear occasionally before the double-noted call begins. His song commences soon afterwards.)

It is usual for each Blackbird's song to consist of many different original tunes with sometimes a few imitations from neighbours of the same species. But a bird living over the fields opposite my garden composed one beautiful melody and sang it exclusively the whole season, never varying this tune or attempting to sing anything else. His constant repetition never jarred for he sang the lovely melody so perfectly. Towards the end of the season another Blackbird added this tune to his own collection and the following spring it was echoed by a dozen more, within a mile radius, perhaps some of his offspring. Not one imitator really got the spirit of this melody, it was a lame affair interpreted by them in comparison to the composer. I have often noticed that Blackbirds sing their own compositions much more expressively than those they crib from neighbours.

As mentioned in the last chapter, the less gifted Blackbirds do much cribbing. For instance, Thief and two others were bad composers, their original efforts were without shape or rhythm, and I could not find a single phrase that could be put into notation because the material was too indefinite. It consisted of one or two notes with a finale comparable to a high-pitched falsetto of a short chuckle-note, or that type of unmusical invention. These birds had some good tunes in their song, but they were cribbed from the Blackbirds named Fields, Blackie, Darky, Oakleaf, etc., and sung badly in comparison to these composers' performances. Listening to the latter four Blackbirds, I could fill a page with the original tunes of each bird and know that they were not imitations, because I had followed their way of composing and knew all the birds intimately. Very occasionally these good singers included an imitation in their song, but this was exceptional, the main bulk of their music was entirely original. Darky has taken an idea from Fields, but almost at once the idea was altered and made into an original variation and later discarded. An especially good melody may be taken up by any singer and when distinguishing an individual by song it must be taken into account that Blackbirds imitate each other's tunes sometimes so that much of the material in a song must be recognised before certainty of the individual can be established. They do not imitate songs of other species.

SONG-THRUSH

The high-voiced, spirited song of the Thrush is very different from the music of poetical moods sung by the mellow-voiced Blackbird. A Thrush, when at work finding food or nesting, is a gentle, retiring bird; often so slow to move, he seems dreaming or half-awake. All the more wonderful is the contrasting character of his song, when perched high on a favoured tree-top, head upturned to heaven, he shouts aloud in clear ringing tones his vigorous notes. A song full of life and energy that can cheer the dullest days, for he sings in November, December and January as well as in nesting months, giving fresh heart to the listener longing for spring.

The Thrush's gift lies in his power as a performer; his short, clean-cut phrases depend for their beauty upon the spirited rhythmic delivery and lovely tone of his voice, the impression being how finely he sings more than how fine his song. As with most of the best singers, some individuals are incomparably superior to others.

Many Thrushes include imitative notes in their song, not only of other species, but of sounds that take their fancy. One gave a clever imitation of my lawn-mower, another produced a rhythmical hammering phrase that appeared to be copied from hearing a roof being tiled. Their choice of imitation from other birds is of rhythmical calls such as Tits, Nuthatch or Woodpecker and some of the Nightingale's forceful notes.

Their quiet subsong consists of many phrases and notes strung together without pause – as with the Blackbird's subsong. Sometimes, with both species, it includes a new phrase that the bird has not sung in full song and, as if practising it for performance later, this is repeated many times over without break, often the whispered tones suddenly giving way to a louder trial of the tune, as if the bird wanted to hear how it sounded in full voice. Young Thrushes and Blackbirds, also some other species, begin singing a simple subsong when a few weeks old; later they select bits from this subdued singing and in louder tones practise them for public performance. Their voice production and technique soon improves, and they gradually add more tunes, giving their voice full play.

MISTLE-THRUSH

The beautiful tone quality of the Mistle-Thrush's voice has a little resemblance to the Blackbird, but less depth and variation. It has the throaty sound of a tenor or viola, less brilliant than the Song-Thrush, but strong and rich within its own more limited register.

Being a rover by nature, his song-perches are often two or three fields apart, usually the topmost branches of certain tall trees, the sound of his plain-song carrying far in leafless days. His song ceases soon after the trees are in leaf. He sings in a bold and direct manner, this wild music of simple line and firm strength seeming the embodiment of sincerity and truth.

Mistle-Thrushes occasionally sing quiet phrases, that may contain imitations of other species, between their full-voiced song. The fledgling-cry is a high-pitched edition of the adult's churring note – which gives him the title of 'Schreecher,' among many countryfolk. This note seems to serve many purposes. I notice when alarmed the tone of their 'churr' becomes harsher, and different inflections of tone quality can often be detected.

In early autumn it is interesting to watch the roving parties of old and young birds together. One September I saw an assembly of eleven in a long, very narrow field bordered with many trees. One bird appeared to be leader, he always perched most prominently on the tallest tree-tops, churred loudest and kept flicking his wings. Two others kept his side of the field, each perched behind him on a different tree, the rest were on the opposite side, also perched apart on bushes and trees. The leader flew forward to the next tree-top and the rest moved up correspondingly, all perching facing the leader, who also faced them while vigorously flicking his wings and churring. Then the bird on the tree behind him flew to his tree, instantly two birds from the opposite side began churring, and also flew to this tree, at which the leader became very excited, turned round on his perch while wing flickering and calling loudly. All were so absorbed that I was able to walk very close to any of them without their seeming to be aware of my presence. It was either some kind of ceremony or a game.

Blackbirds include something of the sort among their many

pastimes. Often a female is the prominent bird who leads off the ceremony – or game – by perching conspicuously on a tree-branch, while wing-flickering and calling, 'Schreeeee' – a note used only for certain occasions (see page 152). At her call other Blackbirds of both sexes gather on her tree, gazing at her while she turns her back to them and flicks her wings. I have seen fourteen Blackbirds, many first-year but some older ones, collect to the tree, keeping as far apart as possible, but all watching the female intently and occasionally answering the 'schreeeee' in a mysterious tone of voice, unlike her vigorous summoning call. Sometimes a male is the prominent bird. These ceremonies may have something to do with pairing; it may be that the leading bird is playing the part of instructor to first-year birds.

To return to the Mistle-Thrush, I have noticed this species has become much scarcer of recent years. Also the 'storm-cock' is now seldom heard singing through wild weather in my district. A Mistle-Thrush nested in my garden for some years and I found it was the Song-Thrushes who sang through bad weather, not my Mistle-Thrush. On fine November or early December days both sang, the Song-Thrush fairly frequently, the 'storm-cock' a very little. Song-Thrushes continued all winter unless there was prolonged snow or frost. My Mistle-Thrush and others in the district stopped singing in mid-winter, starting again about the first or second week of February.

NIGHTINGALE

Although the Nightingale sings by day he needs the mystery of night for his song. He is a great dramatic singer, with more technical ability than any other species. His mysterious note, repeated on a crescendo, is both wonderful for its emotional effect and for masterly control of technique. The poise of that first suspended note has much of the mystery and remoteness of stars on a still summer night; from these heights the dramatist, with his intense vitality, brings the song back to earth by a contrasting brilliant display of dynamic rhythm; heard close, the effect being one of powerful mechanism. Forceful rhythmic phrases and bubbling trill crescendos are performed with amazing skill and driving power, the bird's vitality seeming inexhaustible. There is hardly a moment's break between these phrases; then comes a longer pause, a pause that is part of the song, when the stillness and beauty of night are felt with growing intensity, then the wonderful note is heard and it seems sprung from the poetry of night.

Imagining that note in the hands of a Willow-Warbler, one feels the poetic beauty would be held all through the song, but a Nightingale has other ideas of getting effects, he is a brilliant performer and brings his powerful voice and masterly technique much into play. Each individual does not compose his own tunes – as do the Blackbird and both Thrushes; the material of their song is common to the species. Individuals put some variation in how they sing the set phrases.

ROBIN

In style, Robin music is romantic and rather florid. His voice can be sweet and his subsong is especially charming. When he uses song for disputing with other Robins his timbre often becomes shrill and he distorts phrases that in gentler moods are sung musically. Especially in autumn territorial battles, when song seems used as a language, certain phrases sound threatening, abusive, triumphant, etc.; according to how the battle with his opponent progresses. This may sound anthropomorphism, but it is a fact that one can tell without looking when the invading Robin is giving trouble and follow much that is happening by the sound of the song – the voice, phones, phrases used, and accentuation of certain notes in these phrases.

Although most of the song is common to the species considerable variation occurs with some individuals. Occasionally imitative notes can be detected – from other species – such imitations most often included in the fascinating flow of murmured subsong. Listening intently to one Robin, I heard what sounded like faint echoes of a few notes of Linnet, Goldfinch, Blackcap, Thrush, Great Tit and Blackbird's chuckle-note, all these interspersed without break into the running stream of subsong. So rapidly and smoothly did the song flow that one was only conscious of these imitations by intense concentration, for they were woven among the rhythms of Robin's own song. The clever blending of miniature imitations within his own rhythms made the especial beauty of this bird's subsong.

To me, the music of running brooks and fast-flowing hillside streams is suggested by Robin's subsong. Long ago, before humans built houses and handled a spade for his benefit, he perhaps sought the sheltered streamside banks for territory, for Robins seem bred to the art of fishing. I have seen one fly out to a floating reed on a pond, and from this unstable perch spear food from the water with all the skill of a water-bird, but I was not able to see what he caught. Another time, when I threw bread on a lake for the Waterhens, a Robin flew out, and perching precariously on weed, fished out some of the bread as if he was a born fisher. Most birds who are not waterside species do not show this deftness on the water.

When singing this whispered subsong, Robins often close their eyes and the sound seems to come from far away. At other times they may turn their head from side to side while singing this almost inaudible song, with the air of a public speaker addressing an audience. Sometimes, too, their head-feathers are slightly raised, but there is no other Robin in sight or anywhere near, nor is the display aimed at me, for I have noticed it when I am inside the cottage, and the Robin just outside.

Except in subsong Robin is not a good imitator, although a few individuals sing short cadences resembling notes of some Warblers, and in exceptional cases – as with 'Blackcap Robin' – really good imitations form part of the song to the exclusion of Robin tunes. Attempts to copy other species seem to show up the limitations of Robin's voice, making it sound high-pitched and thin. He has cultivated a decorative style of technique suitable to his timbre and when he tacks these Robin frills on to some imitations they sound out of place – feeble in effect. For instance, if he tries a Tit's song, which depends upon freshness of voice and spontaneous-sounding rhythm, his voice sounds thin and whiny, his rhythm weak and indecisive compared to the Tit. Possibly he is aware of failure, anyway he quickly smothers his effort by a sad-sounding trickle of falling intertones, making a laughably unsuitable ending to the Tit's joyful phrase. Similarly, he makes a hash of the Goldfinch's gay music by falling into a minor key – a mournful streak in Robins being their persistent use of a minor key. (I mean in effect, for literally our major or minor mode is not applicable to bird-music of Robin and Goldfinch.)

I have so far found female Robins sing less full song than males and their song and voice is inferior. Some females sing more subsong, but the quality is not as good. They sing most in autumn when first settled in their territory and do not of course sing at all while nesting.

BLACKCAP

There is no music more lovely than the Blackcap's song. One day, in early June, a Blackcap was singing on the verge of a little wood where white-willows and ash trees blend their soft greens with the deeper shades of alder and oak. At first he flitted from tree to tree, his clear silvery notes, in short phrases, seeming flung to the air as lightly as the wind tossed the willow's long silvery leaves. Then he sang his full song, perched low on a branch with head upturned to the sunlit foliage, and it seemed the bird and the trees were inseparably linked in one great harmonious inspiration. Together they expressed to perfection the music of colour and sound, for the windswept leaves in the sunlight were continually weaving fresh patterns of tone-colour that seemed a complete counterpart to the Blackcap's beautifully woven song. Phrases that began delicately were worked up to a finish on a gust of impetuous force, then a subdued, undulating song with notes flowing faster, until the finely turned fall of the cadence.

Close beside the wood was the Kingfisher's pool, where bright blue dragon-flies darted over the water like sparks struck from the Kingfisher. From the trees above the pool came the slower, deeper notes of a Blackbird. When Blackcap and Blackbird are heard together in full voice there seems no resemblance between their songs – the smaller bird naturally moulds his music on finer lines. But the quality of his song as a Warbler species corresponds with the Blackbird's as a Thrush species. Both are lovers of a tune on large lines. Blackcaps do much finely-woven warbling, but the greatest part of their song is when they break through this into a lovely, ringing tune. This may be sung without preliminary, but they often get a wonderful effect by working up their song, the big melody being held in reserve for the climax.

The subsongs of Blackcap and Thrush tribes have some similarity in mode of expression. One September a Blackbird and Blackcap, perched a little apart, were singing subsongs. The latter included imitative phrases among his own warbles, linking all together and singing in subdued tones until he sang a Blackbird imitation twice, with raised voice and timbre so exactly like a Blackbird singing softly that it seemed the two birds had suddenly changed places. He resumed the subdued tones, but every time the Blackbird imitations were sung he broke into a louder voice. I think this was not in compliment to the nearby Blackbird but because he liked singing the tune and it suited him, for I have at other times heard emphasis given to Blackbird imitations as if they had special appeal. A Song-Thrush may also be well imitated, but his sharper rhythms seem less often favoured.

GARDEN-WARBLER

The Garden-Warbler's long-sustained warbling song is beautiful and rich in trills, but he has not the Blackcap's lovely melody or clear, silvery tones. Many people seem to have difficulty in distinguishing between these two species. There is some resemblance in the warbling part of a Blackcap's song to the Garden-Warbler's luscious, more trilly music, but the latter has not the fine tune referred to above, which Blackcaps sing with such abandon and is really the greater part of their song. There is nothing resembling this in the Garden-Warbler's music. He has concentrated entirely upon rich, decorative warbling, this being much like his subdued, continuous song we term subsong. Exactly where subsong ends and full song begins is difficult to define with some species.

WHITETHROATS

The two Whitethroats, besides their main song, have a varied, long-sustained warbling on the same lines as a Garden-Warbler, but inferior in quality. It is unsatisfactory to call this subsong, for it may be sung quite loudly and is more musical, both in composition and tone quality, than their more dramatic and better-known performances. The shy and charming Lesser Whitethroat has a surprisingly loud, bubbling trill, all on one note, for his main song, attached to a quieter prelude, sung from cover of hedgerows or low bushes. This prelude is really part of the sustained song just mentioned; the length varies and may be anything from three soft notes to a long warble, worked up to a crescendo from almost a whisper. The loud rattling trill may also be heard without any prelude, especially late in the season.

The Greater Whitethroat's best-known song is his flight-dance tune, when he leaps high above the hedgerow, straight and quick as an arrow, dancing down again to the light, springy rhythm of a short song, rather scratchy in tone compared to his long-sustained warbling. As with many species, the fledgling-cry is a sharp double-note, 'chik-ka, chik-ka, chik-ka, chik-ka,' jerked out with sharply-accented rhythm, which suggests the bird is dancing up and down on springs. This fledgling-cry soon grows loud and is full of vitality; already the springy rhythm seems closely related to the adult's song-dance tune. One feels the notes have only to be freed from their monotonous pitch to be irresistibly suitable for the accompaniment of flight. In the mature song the fledgling-cry is noticeable.

Their long-sustained warbling song sometimes contains many imitative notes.

WOOD-WARBLER

Listening to the Wood-Warbler's trill song without seeing his accompanying flight is like hearing Schubert's songs without the piano accompaniment upon which the beauty of the vocal part depends. Yet too often this bird is hidden from view, for his flight-song is set among leaf-covered trees, a sublimely graceful aerial glide timed to the tense rhythm of quickening notes which, as he alights, are resolved into the trembling motion of a trill. This fine trill is uniquely sung on a curve which heightens expression and gives to the straight line of the song — all on one note — the rounded cadence it needs. The following is a diagram of the song:

The sinuosity of the curve is very variable. This song is often repeated many times, only a momentary pause between the repeats. Without seeing the flight it sometimes begins to sound rather mechanical, then comes a wonderful change. There is a short pause and another most beautiful song is intoned, just one note of strangely appealing tone quality, many times intoned on a persuasive rallentando. The earnestness of this song is deeply moving. The bird remains perched while singing with head upraised and sometimes when the song ceases he turns his head searchingly this way and that, as if expecting some effect from his song. He then resumes the flight-song for a while, until again the deeper note is intoned, This song is precious, there is no repetition as with the trill-song.

REED-WARBLER

Heard at his best the Reed-Warbler is among the most wonderful of bird musicians. A good singer has endless variety of effect, he works up great crescendos and his imitations are so well blended into his own rhythms that his song always sounds strikingly original. It varies much with individuals, some being far better songsters than others.

I first heard his song in ideal surroundings at a lake where a Black Tern halts for a few days on his migratory passage both in spring and autumn, and the following extract is from notes made at the time:

Water lilies have now spread their white and golden cups on the smooth surface of Lye Mere and among them Great Crested Grebes have built their island nest. In company with Coots, both parents and young are floating lazily around; the Coots rap out their metallic note, which rings sharply, now loud and close then like an echo faintly sounding in the distance. Two Herons, like age-old guardians, stand high on a forked branch of an old tree overlooking the lake. From the reed-bed far across the mere comes the throbbing of a rhythmic song, suggesting a wild barbaric dance in drum-beat rhythm of primitive tribes. A Willow-Warbler is singing in the trees beside the lake; there is striking contrast in the music of these two birds. The Willow-Warbler's restful song is smoothly rounded, his voice pure-toned and sweet all through the song. The Reed-Warbler's restless music is of an angular type and although there are many lovely-toned, concordant phrases, the pulsing note is often harsh in tone. This rhythmic reiteration of angular or discordant notes gives a wild energy to his song, the rhythm also suggestive, in miniature, of music by certain modern composers who sometimes revert to percussion effects of primitive drum-music.

An example of a Reed-Warbler's rhythm is given on page 141.

SEDGE-WARBLER

To me, the Sedge-Warbler's music is less original and not so strong in effect as the Reed-Warbler's. Most of the Sedge-Warbler's phrases are imitative and he does not usually blend his mimicry into such a well-balanced song sounding like a composition of his own. He seems to be deliberately caricaturing the originators of his imitations as if doing a comic turn, with generous encores for favourite items! I have, however, heard some very finely-balanced, musical song from Sedge-Warblers soon after their arrival, and I think this species becomes more of a caricaturist under the excitement of territorial defence. He is a delightful bird to watch under stress of nesting affairs, when from the top of a reed stem he hurls at his opponent, the Reed-Warbler, a volley of excitable song, phrases and scold-notes culled from a dozen species and sung with exaggerated emphasis.

CHAPTER 12

Songs of Tits, Finches, Pipits, etc.

BLUE TIT

Blue tits have three main songs, one of them often sung with a gliding flight resembling the Wood-Warbler's aerial glide. The songs vary considerably in detail with the individual; the lesser-known one is, I think, what I call the fledgling-cry tune – for Blue Tits are generally thought to have only two songs. This tune consists of the double-noted fledgling-cry several times repeated in joyful manner and strung together in many changing rhythms, varying in length according to the rhythmic pattern. The effect is a roundelay of many fledgling-notes which follow on and overlap. Tits are especially devoted parents and, being temperamentally lively and emotional, they show delight and excitement over nesting affairs more than most species. Hearing this song of the Blue Tit, sung at the very top of his voice from the tallest tree-top within sight of his nest while his mate is sitting, it seems he is overflowing with joy while he spins gay music from the notes that will soon be uttered by the coming brood. When his young are hatched this song is not continued.

His mood seems different in his flight-song. He spreads wide his wings and floats down rapturously through the air while a sparking spray of notes fall from him. Some individuals have more than three songs. Both sexes have many call-notes and a scold-note which is much in evidence if anyone unfamiliar approaches their nest. The male also uses his aerial glide without song – it is known as the 'ghost flight' – but I find some individuals always put this flight to music, although the accompanying song is often sung without flight.

GREAT TIT

Great Tits have much variety of song and conversational notes which are used for certain occasions. Some are common to the species but many are individual inspirations, for this bird is strongly individual in all his ways and full of invention. Sometimes he will take it into his head to give an excellent imitation of another species – Wagtail, Thrush, Hedge-Sparrow, Blackcap, or whatever takes his fancy for the moment. This imitation is generally not repeated. Watching the bird singing his imitation, he occasionally seems doing it for fun and his performance may have an audience of several other birds who hover around, gazing at him while he repeats the imitation many times running, with head and neck outstretched in humorous attitude, and in dancing manner hopping backwards and forwards from one twig to another. He appears to be playing the fool and enjoying himself immensely while the audience watches with interest. This happens in autumn when Tits mix together amicably, and often invent ways of passing the time. Once this performance is over the audience disperses and the imitation is not again repeated.

The phones of many Great Tit phrases stand out clearly like words. As a greeting among themselves and to me, they call 'Hee-hoy.' Those that know me well often call this when meeting me along the road; if I don't stand still and look at them they repeat it loudly and persistently until I do take notice. But if this fails to attract attention the female gives a scold-note; the male more often tries one of his other very dominant-sounding phrases. One day I was gardening when a Great Tit tried to attract my attention by flitting about in front of me with call-notes. Not wanting to stop work and put muddy hands into my pocket for his tit-bit box I pretended not to see him and kept my eyes on the ground. But a Great Tit is never at a loss unless frightened. In a few moments I heard a Wagtail's double-noted call coming from just above my head. Astonished at the perfection of the imitation, I immediately looked at the Tit – he had won, he nearly always does! With airy confidence, suggesting slight swagger, he perched on my hand to eat his tit-bit. I never heard that Wagtail note from him again, it was his inspiration of the moment and done to force my attention.

One delightful song, common to the species, has an accompaniment of wing tremolo – the same kind of ecstatic tremulous movement as in a Lark's soaring flight, only the Tit remains on his perch for the performance. This song, in effect, is slightly like the sound produced by quickly and lightly running a finger backwards and forwards across the strings of a guitar – only, of course, much higher pitched – and there is a slight breath taken before the reverse movement, which gives the song a rocking rhythm of great fascination to me. It is always sung from cover – under a bush, among foliage, or from underneath a chair in my room sometimes. But this, like their other songs, varies in details of intervals, etc.

The well-known 'tee-chū' song has much variation among individuals, each bird sticking to his own version. Here are two examples (Twist's mate's song and Timpano's song):

These songs rapidly and continuously repeated with much verve.

Another song common to Great Tits is:

Whatever his tune he makes the notes ring with life and good cheer.

Young Great Tits in summer and autumn sing a soft, continuous song, a little resembling the Robin's subsong. It is a pity adult Great Tits discard this lovely little song. Females share in some of the conversational notes or phrases and the gentle-toned long spun call-notes she utters when shepherding her young make as charming a piece of music as can be heard from any bird. Although its gentle delivery makes it completely different from any of the other songs, it is a form of miniature representation of the above notation.

Last summer when I was sitting in the orchard listening to a Blackcap singing from the hedge, the Great Tit Inkey flew up to me to get cheese for his young; he perched on my hand and was about to take food when he suddenly drew back, looked towards the warbling Blackcap and remained transfixed in an alert, listening pose, his eyes on the warbler. Then, instead of taking the cheese he flew to a branch beside me and sang an excellent imitation of the Blackcap's warbling. He repeated it several times, then shaking his feathers, as if to throw off the music, he returned to duty, took the cheese and fed his young. I never heard him sing that song again, it had taken his fancy for the moment and it was the rhythm he imitated so well, getting it almost exact only with a little more accentuation of beats. This was no mean achievement, for the Blackcap's warbling is intricate.

Great Tits seems to share one or two phrases with Marsh-Tits, for these are included in the repertoire of both species.

MARSH-TIT AND COAL-TIT

Marsh-Tits and Coal-Tits have several song-notes common to their species, also a variety of phrases are heard from individuals that are totally unexpected. Especially this applies to Marsh-Tits, who may spring a surprise on the listener by a fine, bold imitation of another species. The following unusual incident occurred on April 7th, 1948. (I quote from notes made on the spot.)

From where a Nightingale nests each year a Marsh-Tit sings two of his song-phrases, a trill-note and the loud note that increases in speed until a vibratory effect is achieved. The Marsh Tit's power in this imitation is amazing. He repeats these Nightingale phrases many times from a high tree-branch, with much wing-flickering. He then sings his own songs in his ordinary tones of voice while flitting about the tree. He calls 'Fitz-e-deu, fitz-e-deu,' two or three times, and says 'Bubble-na-na-na.' He has a lot of song today. Then he flies to the tree-top again for the Nightingale notes, ten times more loudly sung than his own songs and the timbre completely different. An astonishing performance for a Marsh-Tit. It actually deceived me at first, for migrants were early that year, Chiffchaff singing on March 7th, Willow-Warbler on 23rd, and I was expecting an early Nightingale. I accounted for the voice sounding not in good form by imagining the bird had just arrived and might be tired after his travels! This is the only time I remember being deceived by an imitation, and it is curious that the Marsh-Tit, who has no reputation for being an imitator, should be the deceiver. But individuality among birds is so strong that they are for ever overstepping their reputations and putting wrong all formulated theories.

CUCKOO

The Cuckoo sings his name in any interval from a second to a fifth. I think each bird generally keeps to his own interval but, when under excitement of pursuing the female, stammering often occurs and other variations of the normal song. It is said, 'In June the Cuckoo changes his tune.' I think it is emotion more than calendar dates that make changes temporally take place. However, the most striking change in tune I have heard was both in June and under excitement. On June 11th the two Cuckoos that had been constantly in the neighborhood of my garden were joined by a third one. The three birds for the next three days behaved very excitedly, displaying and giving chase while uttering odd gutteral notes. One bird continually sang this song, with its two unusual phones and changes of interval.

I came to the conclusion the third bird was a female, this song being sung by the male who had previously haunted my garden, for the other two had no 'Cuckoo' song. The bubbling note was sometimes heard and other odd sounds such as Cuckoos make under excitement of their changeling escapades. After June 14th no Cuckoos were again seen near my garden.

I once saw a female Cuckoo fly to a tree-top with her bubbling note, and perching on a prominent fork of a dead branch, perform actions of nest-building on the bare fork. She turned round very slowly, pressing her breast on the fork exactly as if moulding a nest, sometimes standing up and making actions with her beak as if arranging nesting material round the nest-cup. Her mate watched from a hedge nearby. Presently he began calling and flew to her, perching on one fork-tip. She continued nest-moulding movements, he began displaying in usual Cuckoo fashion. Then he flew off, she following. A few minutes later they returned to the hedge where he had before perched while watching her. As they were often near the same hedge afterwards I am sure some nest there became the first egg depository, for this was early in the season. I was unable to follow up close observations owing to the farm owner objecting to bird-watching on his land.

BULLFINCH

Bullfinches have an original song of a style quite unlike any other species. I believe each individual sings a slightly different tune. The following beautiful little chant was sung by Chanter in my orchard. It was possible to notate it because he used the human scale correctly and had a sense of key, for there is a definite feeling of progression to the tonic — or keynote.

Sung in April:

Sung in May:

He repeated these two notes ⟨music⟩ as if he had satisfaction in his cadence which ⟨music⟩ ends on the keynote. Often he piped this cadence alone — as do other Bullfinches. Sometimes he sang only the first half of the tune, and he gave me the delight of hearing his full chant only a few times, always between 1.30 and 2 p.m. (Summer Time). He also made some other variations of the tune later in the year and the following year.

It is a great pity Bullfinches are lazy over singing their full song since they can compose such good music. It is usual for them to pipe bits of their song as they move about the trees, and their way of doing this reminds me of people who hum fragments of tunes absent-mindedly while going about their work.

Another Bullfinch in my garden sang the same sort of melody, but inserted a double-noted call-note instead of the rests, which gave a very different effect to the song. The first tune (Chanter's) was better music from a human standard because there the bird seemed to have realised that rests in musical phrases are sometimes as important as notes. Filling up gaps with call-notes is decorative, but musically not so strong, although the female Bullfinch perhaps would not agree!

Their piping notes have a distinct resemblance to pan pipes, very softly blown. Bullfinches unfortunately have a rather hesitant delivery which does not do full justice to their compositions. If they had stronger voices and more rhythmic delivery they would truly be great and famous as songsters. But their soft tones are lovely and watching this charming bird while he pipes his plain-song is one of the really great pleasures of life.

LINNET

It seems incomplete to write of the Linnet's song without mention of his mate for he sings his 'love-song' to her during nesting in a more pointed manner than most species. It is very pretty to watch. The following account is of a pair quite fearless of my presence, so very close watching was easier than in some cases.

Two Linnets flew out of a gorse bush, keeping close together and twittering softly. They alighted on the slopes near their chosen bush, the female collecting nesting material while her mate followed behind, not working himself but watching her and seeming to notice all her movements with great eagerness. When her beak was stocked he accompanied her back to the nesting bush; while she started to build he perched close by and, with the sun lighting his crimson breast and crown, he sang a mysterious musical language of phrases half-whispered, half-sung, intermingled with bell-like trills and wistful-sounding, caressing notes. The female often paused in her work to look up at him. The song rose to a fuller, more sustained trill and before this subsided both Linnets again took to the wing, with lilting flight and song. Thus the nest was built, the male always following close behind his mate and singing nearby while she worked. When she brooded the four eggs in her neat little nest, he always faced her while singing continually from perches visible to her. The nest was rather exposed from above and, when the downy grey nestlings felt the sun's heat, their mother perched on a twig jutting over the nest and spread her wings as a sunshade over the brood, her mate supplying food and full measure of song. But a Jackdaw spotted the nest and one morning the poor Linnets were fluttering over the gorse bush, searching and crying for their lost young. The whole morning they cried, hovering over their bush, a piteous sight to watch. Then the male began singing, his voice louder and fuller than before, and in response to his song the mother bird abandoned her search and flew to him; with twittering notes, they remained on the bush a while, then suddenly rose of one accord and with eager, purposeful flight, left the scene of their loss, never to return. Wisely, they had chosen to seek another site for their second brood.

The Linnet's music has much variety of tone colour, from the softest of delicate notes to the brilliance of trill crescendos. When, in flocking season, numbers gather to sing in chorus the concerted effect of rise and fall of tone is very wonderful, and it seems the Linnets do their utmost to produce this effect. It is interesting to watch and listen to flock performances. They may begin by about thirty birds flying to a tree in an excited, purposeful manner, all alighting simultaneously and near together. Then one bird starts singing, by about his third note another joins in, the rest following in quick succession, perhaps six at a time entering the chorus, some trilling, some twittering, some singing upward and downward slurred notes until all voices combine in a great crescendo held for a few moments. Then the volume of tone gradually sinks while over the fields another flock is seen heading in rushing flight for the Linnets' tree. They settle beside the singers and now the chorus again swells, the two flocks by degrees uniting in song until every bird has joined in a redoubled crescendo. The sound of this chorus travels far, stirring other flocks feeding in more distant fields. Before long there is another hurried rushing of wings, and the tree, bare of leaf, becomes laden with Linnets on every twig, all voicing their loudest fortissimo. The song reaches its climax which is held for a time, then the tone falls and rises again, until suddenly, all together, the birds take to flight, their minds tuned to one accord in song now act under one impulse to fly. The deserted tree, standing naked, seems strangely silent and bereft of life.

The Linnets' gradual entry into the chorus is undoubtedly for the purpose of working up a crescendo since these effects of crescendo and diminuendo play a large part in bird-song.

SPARROWS

In autumn large flocks of House and Tree-Sparrows congregate for singing in chorus. Naturally, a rough-toned result is produced from their harsh, chattering notes, but at least they seem striving for an effect of volume of tone. Unlike Linnets, their unruly natures are unable to concentrate long upon music, for throughout the chirruping chorus many ugly squawks can be heard as some members of the choir roughly peck their neighbouring singers in an attempt to bag their perches. Sparrows always want what the other fellow possesses, even if it is the twig upon which he stands! Their chirping chorus is a better musical effort than the solo chatter or chirrup, which can hardly be called song.

GOLDFINCH

The song of a Goldfinch is a musical picture of himself; full of gay charm and brilliance artistically blended with quiet tones; light, quick and spontaneous in movement, lively and light-hearted in effect. Thrush, Blackbird or Blackcap sing with head raised to heaven, not calling attention to their fine feathers while lost in song, but the Goldfinch makes sure the bright colours he wears are seen while singing his full song from a tree-top in spring. Bending low, he rotates his head to show off his crimson head-dress; still singing, he turns round on his perch, slightly spreading his wings so the gold bars he possesses are seen while he works up the trills of his song to a suitable brilliance.

Like most species, his song is fullest in spring, but Goldfinch's fluent, gay music can be heard all summer and autumn, then doubly precious because bird-song has become scarce. They give an impression of happiness perhaps more than any other species; all their actions seem set to music, for their call-note, repeated continually by young and old, is daintily musical and a pleasure to hear. The phones of this call-note sound something like 'wait-a-bit, wait-a-bit,' and often these words seem fitting, especially in flight when they look as if trying to catch up each other by taking light, springy air-leaps while calling 'wait-a-bit, wait-a-bit.'

Young birds, called 'grey-pates,' soon begin to practise their song, at first rather scratchy and unsteady in tone, but they work hard, perched high in some quiet corner, refining their tone quality and by degrees adding more notes to their song.

A charm of Goldfinches will sometimes alight on a tree-top and perform part singing. Their idea of concerted singing seems different from Linnets'. Each bird accentuates his phrasing, phones and cadences so the different voices stand out clearly in counterpoint. This part-singing seems to be intentional and is unlike the sound made when a number happen to be singing between feeding on wayside thistles. Listening yesterday to this part-singing, the following phrase – usual to Goldfinches – was very prominent from one bird:

It sounded most effective against the quick-noted passages and trills of the other birds. They had learnt the value of making short rests all together after cadences, this perhaps being the most definite proof that they were making music together in sympathetic accord, not each bird singing his own song as a solo performance.

The Goldfinch's song is sometimes described as resembling that of a Canary, but Goldfinch music, like his personality, is far daintier than the Canary's.

GREENFINCH

The Greenfinch should take some tips from Goldfinches especially on daintiness! His sturdy full song, heard at its best early in the season, is pleasantly musical, but he soon gets lazy and stolidly grinds out, monotonously as a pedlar calling his wares, the least musical part of his song – two or three notes ending in ' breeeese.'* As the season advances, he cuts out all notes except 'breeeese,' which is persistently repeated in a voice grown coarser and more drawling. This peculiarity may arise from a cumbersome trait in his character, shown when he becomes fearless and intimate on the bird-table, but it is a pity he gets into this rut of droning the least musical portion of his song when possessing trills and other musical notes that are very pleasant to hear. In early spring he sometimes sings while hovering over tree-tops or bushes.

One of his call-notes is a neat little trill which varies in length. When nest-building both male and female extend it considerably and use this note often for calling to each other from the nest; the quick, close trills, held at an even tone level, sound very like electric bells in miniature. When one bird utters the trill-note it never fails to bring a similar response from the mate, either called from a distant bush or while quickly winging towards its mate.

In writing of the Linnet and Goldfinch I mentioned the upward and downward slurred notes in their songs. The Greenfinch's 'breeeese' is drawled up or down, and sometimes drags itself both ways on a droning glissando. This appears to be a Finch-note in common, which each species sings according to his temperament and taste. All three species use the phrase a great deal, both in song and by itself as a solo performance. The Linnet, between his quick passages, often whispers this Finch-note phrase or sings it in the most delicate tones ever uttered by bird, with changing phones for the two notes. Goldfinches sing as if calling brightly:

---

* Handbook's 'Tswee'.

and in each case a glissando up or down is used, sometimes alternating the two, sometimes repeating one way only. This is the same with all three Finches. An apology is now due to Greenfinches for my rudeness over his drawling version of the Finch-note. The Green Linnet is a fine singer at times, and I am very fond of watching this bird.

CORN-BUNTING

I first heard a Corn-Bunting's song one August day when sitting under the lee of a wheatfield on high downland. A strong, gusty wind blew with a cutting sound through the hard, stiff ears of corn; apart from this it was very quiet, and no birds were in sight. Then came a lull in the wind and another sound, unknown to me, came from across the wheat-field. For a moment this, too, seemed the wind playing on the stiff, ripe corn, then I stood up to search the great field for a first glimpse of the bird. He was perched on a tall thistle surrounded by a sea of golden corn, wheezing out his song every second as if breathing life into all the ripening grains of wheat. 'Ticker, ticker, dureees-er; ticker, ticker, dureees-er' – a small sound in the vastness of the open downland space yet it seemed vital heard in that field of growing corn.

Autumn flocking season is another time when this species can be fully appreciated. During September and early October they congregate in large numbers on reedy marshland several miles from my home. A flock of sixty or more will perch on a bush to wind up their little clocks – for so their song sounds. They seem too preoccupied to notice or fear the bird-watcher within about six feet, but one step nearer and a few fly off with their call-note 'ticker, ticker, ticker,' others follow on until all are flying, ticking like a lot of busy wound-up clocks. 'Ticker' is their flock call, but also it often begins their song. Even their flight has a suggestion of clockwork, the whizzing movement of their wings looking like a flywheel spinning round at a tremendous pace, hard pushed to keep the heavily-built body on the move! But the Corn-Bunting, although not a great singer, seems of vital importance to that marshland as in the field of ripening corn.

YELLOWHAMMER

The Yellowhammer's song depends for its beauty upon a wonderful cadence which is not always sung, especially in some northern districts, where I believe the song frequently falls short of its perfection. Perhaps the climate there is less favourable, for this species sings best in warmth and sunshine, choosing mid-morning and afternoon for music and singing all through the heat of summer days.

From some high perch the Yellowhammer sings his little song of a few quick, level-toned notes leading to the cadence of one note poised high and a sheer drop to the final note, this rise and fall of interval very beautiful when the bird sings his best, the good singer putting just the right balance of tone and pronouncing clearly the lovely change of phone on the high note 'no.' The rise and fall of interval and phone-changes are evidently hard to accomplish, and it takes the young bird a long time even to attempt the cadence. The quick opening notes are first sung and after some weeks the high note may be jerked out in clumsy fashion as if the bird found it beyond his technical ability; the last note of sudden fall in pitch is not attempted until the following year. I once heard a young and an adult Yellowhammer singing from adjoining trees. The contrast was interesting. In this case the youngster pitched his song approximately a fifth higher and his immature effort ended on the high note, squeaked out as if his voice had broken. As his song was pitched so high perhaps the top note was beyond the compass of his voice. The mature bird's performance showed what artistic perfection can be reached even in the Yellowhammer's little song.

CURLEW, REDSHANK, ETC.

Birds can create a remote atmosphere just by one or two notes. This applies most of all to the Curlew's lovely call and to his music of crescendos and diminuendos, an air-born song with travelling trills that seem to come from infinity, linking the unknown beauty with all that we know of loveliness. The Redshank's notes and trilling have something of the same far-reaching quality, as also the other smaller Waders, who set the air trembling with their chorus of clear, piping notes while they themselves remain invisible as spirits against the dun-coloured feeding ground until suddenly their music ceases and they appear as one flickering-white form, moving fast above earth – the song-chorus embodied in flock-flight. With electrical precision the flashing white form changes colour to dark grey as it twists and turns rapidly over the feeding ground. Then flight ceases and the fast-moving flock looks to have flown beneath earth, so invisible do the Waders become as together they touch land, again making soft music with their clear, liquid voices that have such a strangely moving quality. The bond between music and flight is strong. Both are arts belonging to the freedom of air and space, both have movement formed into rhythm by balance of time.

TREE-PIPIT

The Tree-Pipit and Meadow-Pipit are among those who combine song with flight, both birds' performances being beautiful, but the Tree-Pipit's music is far richer. His song varies much in beauty for some individuals dispense with the flight; they then sing only a stilted edition of the song, full expression never being reached without the usual combination of flight. The two are so interdependent that the best songs have the best flights. An abridged song is sung to a very short, fluttering rise and gliding return to the same perch, but the flight-song can reach superb perfection.

For me, one individual Tree-Pipit shines out above all others I have heard. It was one spring day when the beech trees on the slopes of Wolstonbury Hill were just ready to break into leaf – a small spray of green showing here and there. From one of these trees rose the small brown bird, the sun lighting his plumage to a bright russet-brown exactly matching the sheaved buds of the beeches, while his pale underparts shone the same colour as the silvery stems of the trees. Like a Sky-Lark he soared on vibrant wings, then in exquisite full song he hovered a moment and floated down on wide-spread wings in a perfect spiral towards another tree, caressingly intoning 'seea-seea-seea,' his notes coming slower, slower, until he alighted with one last lingering 'seea,' then changed his tune to 'e-chuff, e-chuff, e-chuff' – these last notes sounding as if letting out steam after perching. Soon he rose again and many times repeated this perfect flight-song with an aerial curve over the trees, always gliding in caressing song to a different beech. This gave me the fanciful impression he was performing some wonderful rite of blessing the beeches of Wolstonbury Hill while they began to unfurl their leaves. It is a pity this beautiful flight-song is so often abridged by lazy or incompetent performers.

SKY-LARK

The Sky-Lark seems to belong more to heaven than to earth. When he sings near to earth without soaring the song lacks its fervour. Always a wing tremolo – or vibrato – accompanies his flight-song. I have seen a Lark singing his full song facing a strong breeze and drifting slowly backwards on tremulous wings. When the field hedge was below him the song and wing fluttering suddenly ceased, and he flew quickly forward against the wind, with fast but firmly-beating wings alternating between rests with wings closed, a dipping flight accompanied by his call-note, 'seep, seep.' They have a short little song, sung close to the ground or when chasing each other, this seeming conversational and an extension of one of their call-notes – the trill call-note.

Lark music has special significance for me. One of the great experiences of my life was when I first heard the song, at the age of about eleven, with full realisation of its beauty. I was lying on the slopes of a sand-dune, a book opened to start reading, when the Lark's song suddenly held me; while the bird soared far into the sky overhead his music brought a glorious revelation of beauty, not only for its own sake, but because it seemed the true meaning of life. Certain details of the scene remain vividly clear, especially the marram-grass tufts on the high sand-hill above me, the last pinnacle of earth beyond which was the blue sky, the Lark's world.

A bird, in spite of the inspirational power of his song, is generally supposed to be devoid of the immortal soul accredited to man. Among those who feel strongly the spiritual appeal of bird-song there must be some who ponder this question: How can bird-music have this great power to move a human soul unless a bird's spirit, released in song, is component with the Divine?

> The starry voice ascending spreads,
> Awakening, as it waxes thin,
> The best in us to him akin:
>
>   •   •   •   •   •
>
> Our wisdom speaks from failing blood,
> Our passion is too full in flood,
> We want the key of his wild note
> Of truthful in a tuneful throat.

VINTAGE CLASSICS

Vintage Classics is home to some of the greatest writers and thinkers from around the world and across the ages. Bringing you not just the books you already know and love, but new additions to your library, these are works to capture imaginations, inspire new perspectives and excite curiosity.

Renowned for our iconic red spines and bold, collectable design, Vintage Classics is an adventurous, ever-evolving list. We breathe new life into classic books for modern readers, publishing to reflect the world today, because we believe that our times can best be understood in conversation with the past.